PRISONS, PENOLOGY
AND PENAL REFORM

PETER LANG
New York • Washington, D.C./Baltimore • Bern
Frankfurt am Main • Berlin • Brussels • Vienna • Oxford

Curt R. Blakely

PRISONS, PENOLOGY AND PENAL REFORM

An Introduction to Institutional Specialization

PETER LANG
New York • Washington, D.C./Baltimore • Bern
Frankfurt am Main • Berlin • Brussels • Vienna • Oxford

Library of Congress Cataloging-in-Publication Data

Blakely, Curt R.
Prisons, penology and penal reform: an introduction
to institutional specialization / Curt R. Blakely.
p. cm.
Includes bibliographical references and index.
1. Prisons—United States. 2. Imprisonment—United States.
3. Prisoners—United States. 4. Privatization—United States. I. Title.
HV9471.B53   365—dc22   2006025284
ISBN 978-0-8204-8831-8

Bibliographic information published by **Die Deutsche Bibliothek**.
Die Deutsche Bibliothek lists this publication in the "Deutsche
Nationalbibliografie"; detailed bibliographic data is available
on the Internet at http://dnb.ddb.de/.

Cover design by Joni Holst

The paper in this book meets the guidelines for permanence and durability
of the Committee on Production Guidelines for Book Longevity
of the Council of Library Resources.

© 2007 Peter Lang Publishing, Inc., New York
29 Broadway, 18th floor, New York, NY 10006
www.peterlang.com

Printed in the United States of America

To Mary and the Fab Four. May this work inspire each of you.
Possibilities exist if you just believe!

Contents

List of Tables

Foreword

You are about to read a work that is bound to become a standard in the field of penology. Few other books delve into the modern prison in such an insightful manner. None that I am aware of provides a mechanism by which the prison can be made more effective. I have worked in the prison system and have subsequently studied it for years. I can say with a degree of authority that the material contained herein will introduce you to a world that few citizens ever experience and even fewer regularly contemplate. This book reminds each of us about the benefits of a properly working prison system. At the very heart of this book is a genuine interest in the prison, in the inmate, in reform through treatment, and ultimately in ways to make the prison more effective in promoting public safety. All too often books dealing with the prison neglect its traditional objectives and in doing so fail to acknowledge that its ultimate purpose is the promotion of community safety and not merely the containment or punishment of the offender.

One of Dr. Blakely's premises is that the average citizen has largely forgotten the important role that the prison can play in building a safe society. Why have we largely forgotten about the prison? Perhaps for many of us the prison signifies hopelessness and lost innocence. Perhaps it is because we are afraid of those it houses. Regardless of the reason(s), I agree with Dr. Blakely wholeheartedly! We have largely forgotten about the prison—that is, until some headline reminds us of the violence occurring behind its walls or until an ex-inmate commits an unspeakable act. We can no longer afford to ignore one of the most important social institutions of all time. What other institution can promote public safety to the same extent as the prison? In this sense, the prison stands alone. We must not forget this simple fact.

Recently the prison has undergone some monumental changes. Most of these changes have been driven by a growing "get-tough" approach to crime that has resulted in a massive surge of offenders into our correctional institutions. This has led prison officials largely to abandon inmate reform and instead focus their energies on maintaining control of our prisons. The prison is now in crisis and unless it regains its bearings and again recognizes the importance of inmate reform, it may be permanently transformed into little more than a reactionary institution that takes no proactive measures to promote our safety.

Given this, let me explain why this book will become required reading in corrections-related courses. First, it aptly identifies current dilemmas facing the prison. These include well-known but often ignored problems associated with inmate classification. Furthermore, the practice of housing inmates based solely upon security designations often results in losing the impressionable offender to the corrupting influence of the more hardened inmate. Countless numbers of young and salvageable inmates who would have benefited from treatment have been lost to "lives of crime" because of this destructive practice. Those of us who have worked in or around the prison know that salvageable inmates exist. We must target this portion of the inmate population for treatment. After having addressed some of the problems facing the modern prison, Dr. Blakely offers one of the most innovative and progressive solutions I have ever encountered. He calls his solution simply "prison specialization." He gives it no fancy names nor does he try to dress it up in academic regalia. Instead he offers a solution that may prove to be one of the most creative proposals to impact the field of penology in a century.

It would be an injustice to approach this book simply from the viewpoint that it provides a possible solution to the many problems facing the contemporary prison. Instead, as Dr. Blakely notes, its real contribution can be found in its ability to spark debate about how these problems might be addressed. Yes, specialization is offered as a solution to these problems, but Dr. Blakely is wise enough to urge others to find solutions that may prove even more effective. I certainly join Dr. Blakely in this endeavor and hope that penologists nationwide will accept his challenge. The time is right for change within our prisons, and this book will be the spark that drives this reform well into the future.

Vic W. Bumphus, Ph.D.
University of Tennessee at Chattanooga

Preface

The book that you now hold in your hands is the continuation of the work started in an earlier book entitled *America's Prisons: The Movement Toward Profit and Privatization*. Within its pages, readers were introduced to changes that are occurring in our prisons—primarily the adoption of profit as an operational objective and the "closed" approach to prison management that is becoming so popular. By a "closed" approach, I am referring to the growing practice of shielding prison operations from the public's view. This effectively frees correctional officials from their traditional social mandate of promoting public safety and instead permits them to operate institutions that are little more than human warehouses. Not only are prison officials adopting a closed approach to facility operations but they now perceive inmate populations very differently than they were perceived just a few short years ago. Instead of inmates being viewed as individuals, they are now almost exclusively viewed in the aggregate. What this suggests is that inmates have largely been stripped of their individuality. This has resulted in an approach that values the housing of large numbers of inmates without any attempt at salvaging those who are salvageable. The prison has now reached a critical point in its history. We must decide whether we want the prison simply to house offenders or whether it should help produce socially responsible and productive citizens. Such a determination is important since nine out of every ten inmates eventually return to their communities. As we stand at this crossroads, we must decide whether to permit the prison to operate as it is or to take an alternate path. It is the second choice, I believe, that is the correct route—hence the need for this book.

As you read the following pages please remember that the public has an absolute right to expect, and if necessary to demand, that its government act in a manner that promotes its best interests. For the prison to promote the public's interest, correctional officials must realize that there are two types of inmates—those who are best dealt with through containment, and those who are more appropriately dealt with through an intense and meaningful treatment program designed to reform the reformable. While each approach certainly promotes public safety in its own unique way, it is the reformed inmate who reflects more positively upon both the prison and society. What I am suggesting is simple, that prisons specialize in the types of offenders they house. For example, one prison might specialize in housing the hardened offender while another houses the young and impressionable inmate who is an appropriate candidate for intense treatment. The traditional practice of housing these two types of inmates within the same prison is counterproductive and has served to perpetuate crime. This practice unfairly and unwisely places the treatable inmate in a position where he/she must choose either pursuing treatment and potentially becoming the target of unwanted attention by other inmates or shunning treatment in order to fit in with the inmate population. Untold numbers of impressionable inmates have been lost to the criminal element simply because more experienced offenders have gotten to them first. We must break this cycle and strive to reach this population before they are lost forever. Treatment is important for another reason—it reflects a governmental outlook that values human life. The manner in which the government approaches prison inmates (representing the disenfranchised and poor) serves as a barometer for how the government may eventually approach other groups. Therefore, we should always strive to ensure that offenders' constitutional rights are protected and that they are treated humanely. While this book is concerned primarily with the prison and the manner in which its inmates are treated, the ramifications are indeed much broader.

In the pages that follow, you will be introduced to a good deal of correctional theory and thought. This introduction will specifically include a consideration of the objectives of security, rehabilitation, retribution, deterrence, and incapacitation. You will also be introduced to changes occurring within the prison, including a growing de-emphasis on rehabilitation. I will argue that rehabilitation as an operational objective, whether obtainable on a grand scale or not, has a normalizing effect on the otherwise harsh environment of the prison. Without the humanitarian effect of a reform ideology, other ideologies can be freely adopted, many of which fail to take into account the best interests of the inmate or society. If this occurs, we run the risk of increasing the harshness and damaging consequences associated with imprisonment. If we fail to recognize that the prison deals with fragile humans, then the prison will forever remain ineffective in promoting the long-term safety of the citizenry. In addition to improved classification processes and prison specialization you will be introduced to prison privatization. Prison privatization will become an essential ingredient in improving the prison's ability to increase public safety. Personal insight and observation accompany the material presented throughout this book. This insight is used to supplement research findings and at times challenges common misconceptions. Furthermore, "What if?" questions will require the reader to determine whether improvement to the prison system is warranted and what the consequences of changes may be.

Finally, a number of predictions will be made. After all, what good is all this talk about the prison without predictions? As you will see, the predictions appearing in the final chapter portray future prisons as institutions that are little more than efficient human warehouses. But the good news is that it is not too late. There is time to return the prison to its former self, an institution that promotes community safety through inmate treatment.

Acknowledgments

As with most scholarly pursuits that end in the publication of a book, there are always more people involved than just the writer. I trace the heritage of the present work to 1993. It was while I was a student at Central Missouri State University that Professor Allan Sapp helped pique my interest in penology and the underlying objectives driving contemporary prison operations. Of particular interest to both of us was how prison privatization fit into the broader correctional scheme. In essence, we were interested in determining the advantages and disadvantages associated with the private sector prison. I have recently learned that Professor Sapp has since retired from academia and is now enjoying the "good life."

In addition to Professor Sapp, others have influenced me and have helped shape my outlook on the topics of inmate classification, privatization, and specialization. First and foremost is Professor Thomas Castellano. Professor Castellano served as my mentor and dissertation chair during my doctoral years. I tried his patience on many occasions. Yet, even in trying times, he stayed the course—convincing me that perhaps I too should stay the course. Professor Castellano has since left

Southern Illinois University and is currently the Chair of the Criminal Justice Department at the Rochester Institute of Technology.

My first full-time academic job after completing my doctorate was at the University of South Alabama. Here, Dr. Tim O'Shea has assumed the formidable task of serving as my faculty mentor. He continues to provide equal measures of motivation and inspiration. He continually pushes me to write as often as possible. He too has helped shape my outlook and has explained that with a few well-placed modifications, the prison's effectiveness could be substantially improved. It is from these individuals that I have learned my most valuable lessons regarding scholarship, academe, and the responsibility that goes along with teaching. I also gratefully acknowledge the guidance and friendship of Professor Vic Bumphus of the University of Tennessee at Chattanooga. Each of these individuals has my gratitude and respect. I hope that each continues to shape the minds of students just as they have helped shape mine. Perhaps during the course of my own career, I too might influence others in a similar fashion. To do so would certainly signify a degree of personal and professional success.

Finally, I acknowledge the help and support of my family. Without them this project would never have come to fruition. Each has permitted me time to think and write. Often this amounted to substantial personal sacrifice. Furthermore, each has spent untold hours listening to me read and reread the present work—only to be asked "How did that sound?"

Major Assertions Made in This Book

- Rehabilitation instills within the offender a respect for himself/herself, others, and particularly the law.
- The ultimate goal of rehabilitation is to produce a socially responsible and law-abiding citizen.
- A rehabilitative rationale seeks to create a prison experience that is both productive and meaningful.
- Rehabilitation is a largely unexplored objective within the contemporary prison.
- Scholars generally agree that financial factors are the leading obstacle to inmate reform.
- Despite better education and training, many correctional employees remain unaware of the prison's history or traditional objectives.
- A workforce that is unaware of its history is a workforce that is not guided by a sense of professionalism or vision.
- Offenders and nonoffenders are more similar than different.
- Most inmates are young males who are incarcerated in minimum-security prisons. This suggests that they have been convicted of relatively minor offences and show little propensity toward violence.

- Traditionally, an institution's effectiveness was measured in terms of recidivism rates.
- Contemporary incarceration has become little more than human warehousing with few opportunities for self-improvement.
- Today, a prison's capacity largely establishes its social value.
- Recent legislative acts have significantly curtailed the judiciary's ability to oversee prison operations.
- There are two groups of inmates—those who are amenable to treatment and those who are not.
- Only those inmates amenable to treatment can be reformed.
- One of the original purposes of inmate classification was to identify an inmate's needs and then design an appropriate course of action to help the inmate address those needs.
- Classification based upon security and treatment concerns is essential if a prison is to maximize its social value.
- Normalization refers to the prison's attempt to provide a wide range of treatment options and to promote inmate responsibility.
- The contemporary prison is simply the best "college of crime" available to the offender.
- Generalized incarceration cannot meet every inmate's unique needs nor can it fulfill the expectations of most taxpayers.
- Since generalized incarceration is ineffective, prison specialization becomes necessary.
- Prison specialization refers to the creation of specialized prisons designed to house only one particular type of inmate.
- Under prison specialization, inmates are classified according to their desire and ability to undergo treatment.
- Prison specialization seeks to increase community safety through inmate containment and reform.
- Offender treatment is a process that may begin in the prison but must continue after release.
- Treatment and security should no longer be viewed as separate activities but rather as activities with a shared objective—community safety.
- Prison privatization refers to the process by which the government contracts with the private sector to house inmates on its behalf.
- Many early prisons were privately operated.

- The government's monopolization of the pursuit, apprehension, prosecution, and punishment of the offender is a relatively recent development.
- The roots of modern prison privatization can be traced to the 1960s, when social dissent increased throughout the United States.
- Social dissatisfaction with the government has led to criticism of its monopolization of correctional services.
- Kentucky was the first state to partially privatize its prison system.
- Inmates incarcerated in private prisons have often been convicted of relatively minor crimes. Therefore, their sentences are much shorter than the sentences of inmates housed by the public prison.
- The judiciary remains unconvinced that there is a relationship between profit and inmate mistreatment.
- Prison privatization and prison specialization are complementary pursuits.
- The prison's future is not predestined—its path can and should be altered.
- Before the path of the prison can be altered, practitioners must become familiar with its traditional objectives and history.
- While most penologists agree that the prison is in need of change, debate exists about the extent of change needed.
- Reform ideology has a humanizing effect on the prison.
- By failing to recognize the importance of inmate reform, the prison is neglecting its duty to promote public safety.
- Internal measures of prison performance consider characteristics that are largely hidden from the public's view.
- Internal performance measures provide little meaningful information to the average citizen.
- Recidivism is an external performance measure.
- An external performance measure quantifies a prison's achievements in a manner easily understood by the average citizen.
- It is not too late—the prison can be returned to its former state as an institution that focuses upon the individual.

The role of the prison in contemporary society is multifaceted and complex. But the fact remains that the two most important objectives of the prison are the containment **and** *reformation of the offender.*

Chapter One

Prison: One Institution, Many Expectations

I assume that since you are reading this book you are either a student of penology or an interested citizen. Either way you will be introduced to a wide array of information and ideas in the pages that follow. This material for the most part is not available elsewhere. Some of it is based upon findings that appear in *America's Prisons: The Movement Toward Profit and Privatization*—an earlier book in which I explore the contemporary prison and the changes occurring with regard to its operations. All of the material that follows is based in part on common sense, personal observation, and research that spans nearly two decades. This book is a direct attempt to reintroduce penology into the contemporary literature. This statement suggests that the current literature largely ignores ideas and suggestions that could both advance our understanding of the prison and increase its effectiveness. Regardless of the poor state of affairs pertaining to prison-related thought, a renewed interest in penology promises to facilitate discussion about how we might increase the prison's ability to promote public safety. We should no longer ignore the prison as a social institution—out of sight should not necessarily mean out of mind! In fact, where the prison is concerned, such an approach can have devastating effects.

Let us begin with a consideration of penology. **Penology** is simply the study of the prison's operations, its objectives, and those individuals whom it employs and incarcerates. As a recognized discipline, penology emerged in the early twentieth century. Early penologists continually sought new methods to make the prison a more effective social institution. Debate often centered around the role that training, education, punishment, and penitence could play in promoting community safety. At the center of penology is an undeniable interest in

- the offender,
- prison operations,
- methods of treatment, reform, and rehabilitation,
- the evolution and history of the prison, and
- ways to promote community safety.

When we consider these areas of interest, it should become obvious that penology is a progressive discipline. As such, it values prison operations that promote inmate reform and accountability within the broader framework of public safety. Being in a progressive discipline, penologists should ideally seek to maximize the prison's effectiveness, and yet many of our leading penologists fail to endorse reform as a worthy pursuit or an achievable goal. Since many penologists have openly abandoned rehabilitation as an operational objective, other individuals, including practitioners, also hesitate to discuss reform and instead increasingly view containment as the prison's primary goal. Owing to this failure to recognize reform as a worthy objective or to acknowledge the value of penology as a field of study, interest among college students in prison-related careers has waned. This is not to suggest that other factors are not at work, but colleges are currently doing very little to stimulate interest or provide substantive courses on the prison. This is unfortunate since colleges produce graduates who actively avoid corrections as a career choice. In a very real sense the prison is suffering from a "brain drain" that clearly distinguishes it from many other areas within the criminal justice system. My hope is that as criminal justice courses continue to increase in popularity, correctional courses will become more prevalent, drawing greater numbers of students into the corrections field.

Admittedly, as with many individuals who work in prisons, my employment was largely by happenstance. As a college student I neither desired a career in corrections nor foresaw any long-term opportunity within the prison. I considered the prison little more than a refuge for those who simply could not find employment elsewhere. Instead, I spent many hours a day dreaming about my future as either a vice cop or detective. After all, both television and the movies made police work seem exciting. I had grown up watching *Starsky and Hutch*, *Columbo*, *Police Story*, and my all-time favorite, *Miami Vice*. Each of these shows made a law enforcement career appear exhilarating. In an opposite fashion, when prisons were depicted they were always presented as dark, lonely places where brutality and corruption flourished. One need only consider the prison's portrayal in many popular films to understand my point. For example, consider the following movies:

- *The Big House* (1930),
- *Cool Hand Luke* (1967),
- *Brubaker* (1980),
- *Shawshank Redemption* (1994), and more recently
- *The Green Mile* (1999).

Of course, each of these movies, to a varying degree, portrays the prison in a negative fashion. In a similar sense, books also provide imagery that is vivid and thought-provoking. A few of the most acclaimed books that depict the prison include the following:

- *The Devil's Butcher Shop: The New Mexico Prison Uprising* (1988),
- *The Hot House: Life inside Leavenworth Prison* (1993),
- *Slaughter in Cell House 3—The Anatomy of a Riot* (1997), and
- *The Big House: Life inside a Supermax Security Prison* (2004).

If you have seen any of these films or have read these books, you must concede that they portray the prison quite negatively. While not all of this negativity is deserved, it does continue to influence the manner in which the general public views the prison. Once established, a negative image is difficult to escape. This negativity notwithstanding, a few students of criminal justice do, sooner or later, find themselves employed by the prison.

My first position in corrections was as an officer with the Missouri Board of Probation and Parole. Upon assuming my initial duties, I was puzzled to find that I was expected to supervise those on my caseload but not to initiate treatment. I was somewhat confused by this since probation and parole were originally intended to be a corrective and reform-oriented process. While I was initially willing to act as little more than a control agent, I quickly realized that such an approach enabled many of these individuals to continue in their destructive lifestyles. Owing to this view of offenders as individuals in need of control but not treatment, many continued to act in antisocial ways. In essence, I could control their actions to some extent, but knew all too well that this control was short-lived—usually a few years at best. Thus, offenders often completed supervision without addressing their particular problems. These shortcomings made it difficult

- for officers and offenders to discern what objectives (if any) were being pursued
- for officers to recognize and implement intervention strategies, and
- for meaningful assertions to be made regarding supervision's overall contribution to the public's long-term safety.

While many practices adopted by this agency went counter to the public's long-term health, I nevertheless learned the importance of establishing clearly identifiable objectives for the benefit of staff and offenders alike. Furthermore, I also learned that among any offender population there are those who cannot and will not cooperate when given the opportunity to pursue reform. However, there are also those offenders who value reform and have clearly recognized that personal change is needed. Regardless, without offender cooperation and free participation, no amount of coercion or force will produce change.

Following my employment with Missouri, I vowed that I would never again work in the correctional field. I had become disillusioned with the entire correctional profession. But fate had other plans. A friend had spoken quite highly of his experience with the New Mexico Corrections Department, so highly in fact that I soon found myself applying for a position with the **Penitentiary of New Mexico** (PNM) at Santa Fe. I was aware that PNM was the scene of our nation's bloodiest prison riot. I also realized that if I could make it there, I could make it anywhere. I reasoned that PNM's reputation would prove beneficial to me as I continued to cultivate my career—wherever that career might eventually lead.

Built in 1957, the main facility of the Penitentiary of New Mexico until recently served as the state's primary prison. It was originally designed to house just 850 inmates, but often housed considerably more. Over its long and fabled history, PNM garnered a reputation for violence and the use of poor administrative practices. In light of severe overcrowding, staff attempted to maintain institutional control by cooperating with inmate leadership. This cooperation helped provide a small degree of stability to a volatile setting. As the 1970s ended, the relationship between staff and prisoners turned noticeably hostile. Prison officials increasingly used physical coercion, segregation, and inmate informants as methods of maintaining control. Ultimately, these practices produced one of the most unstable prisons in the United States.

On February 2, 1980, the penitentiary was the site of an exceptionally savage riot—the likes of which had never been seen. In a matter of minutes, prisoners were able to overpower correctional officers and gain access to the control center. A prison's **control center** is the location from which all movement can be monitored and managed. Furthermore, the control center generally houses the institution's keys, radios, and weapons. Once the control center was breached, the remainder of the facility succumbed rather quickly. During the 36-hour disturbance, 33 inmates were brutally murdered. Many were tortured savagely before being killed. Some of these bizarre killings were blamed on the consumption of large amounts of medications obtained from the prison's infirmary. Regardless of what may have contributed to the events of that night, 200 more inmates were raped or otherwise brutalized. The cost of facility repair was estimated to be between $70 and $100 million. The State's Attorney General later reported that crowding, understaffed security, correctional officer misconduct, and classification inadequacies were contributory factors. Much of the damage resulting from the riot has never been repaired. During my years at PNM, portions of the facility remained as they had been following the riot. In fact, an entire housing wing had simply been abandoned to the elements of the high desert.

Upon arriving at PNM for my initial interview, I noticed that employees were frequently stopping to pray before entering the institution. This had a chilling effect upon my attitude, since scenes of the 1980 riot (captured on videotape) were continuously playing in my head. I met first with the Deputy Warden. He asked me to explain the difference between minimum-, medium-, and maximum-security prisons and how, in my opinion, each affected the inmate. Following this brief meeting, I then met with the Warden, who also questioned me about the traditional objectives of the prison. My responses must have been satisfactory since I was asked to start immediately. Still today, I too ask my students many of these same questions.

Over the next three years, I noticed, as I had in Missouri, that the correctional system was failing in its mission to reform the offender and in all probability was functioning in a manner that actually discouraged offender reform. It appeared that both Missouri's Board of Probation and Parole and PNM were operating in a manner that helped ensure ease of operations without consideration for the needs or desires of either the offender or society. This led me to again question the overall purpose of corrections and especially the prison. Is the purpose of the prison really to correct and reform the inmate, or is it simply to manage the offender population? I surmised that if the purpose is to correct the inmate, then the system is failing miserably. Such a failure has both personal ramifications for the offender and grave consequences for society.

> *What if . . . officials were to stress offender reform to the same extent that they value ease of operations? Would such a position necessitate changes to the prison itself?*

As you may have gathered, there exist a myriad of opinions about how the prison should be operated. Generally, most views fall into one of two lines of thought. The first takes the position that our prisons are approaching the inmate population too harshly. Those adhering to this perspective believe that we should assist offenders by providing them with counseling, education, and vocational training. Through these programs, the inmate is expected to develop the skills necessary to obtain and maintain employment. Employment is an absolute requisite for a law-abiding lifestyle. If employment is obtained upon release, then it is surmised that the offender will have neither the time nor the inclination to commit additional crimes.

The other line of reasoning views the system as being overly lenient. Those adhering to this perspective seek to implement legislation to create mandatory and lengthy prison terms. This approach stresses punishment, incapacitation, and deterrence while devaluing rehabilitation. Not only do proponents advocate the increased use of the prison, but they also view large inmate populations as a measure of such an approach's effectiveness. Under this approach, inmates are dealt with in the aggregate and not viewed as unique individuals. Likewise, prisons are to be devoid of ordinary comforts and their staff should be cold, uncaring, and detached. Incarceration under this approach is truly "hard time," since few comforts are provided. Since rehabilitation is not valued, the future conduct of the ex-inmate is of little concern and recidivism rates are discounted as a measure of the prison's effectiveness.

Two Lines of Thought Regarding Prison Operations

Those perceiving the prison as overly harsh

- believe that the prison should instead value inmate reform,
- believe that treatment, education, and vocational training should be offered, and
- believe that through education and the development of skills, inmates will be adequately prepared to assume positions of responsibility upon release.

Those perceiving the prison as overly lenient

- believe that the prison should emphasize its punitive nature,
- believe that the prison should provide an environment no better than what is commonly experienced by our poorest citizens (the rationale being that crime should not elevate one's standard of living above what is experienced by even the lowliest law-abiding citizen), and
- believe that such an approach will have a deterrent effect.

Of these two perceptions, it is the one that values a punitive approach that is gaining support. Support for this perspective is based upon the assumption that harsh punishments tend to produce a deterrent effect. **Deterrence** refers to the ability of criminal sanctions to reduce illegal activity. Deterrence is often seen as an objective that is easier and cheaper to achieve than is offender reform. This belief holds that a fear of punishment is always easier to generate than is personal change. Deterrence depends on the fear of detection, prosecution, and punishment, whereas inmate reform relies upon personal growth brought about by education and the development of desirable skills. There are two types of deterrence—specific and general. **Specific deterrence** refers to punishment's ability to discourage further criminal actions by a particular offender, while **general deterrence** refers to punishment's ability to discourage criminality among the general public. In other words, under general deterrence it is the punishment of an individual offender that serves as a warning to all would-be criminals.

The operational objectives of punishment and treatment are reflected in the ideologies of "normalization" and "less eligibility." Under the philosophy of **normalization** inmates are given considerable freedom and are encouraged to make responsible decisions during their term of incarceration. Often responsible decisions pertain directly to an inmate's conduct while incarcerated, his/her participation in treatment programs, and maintenance and cultivation of positive relationships with family, friends, and past employers. It is believed that if inmates make responsible decisions while incarcerated, they will be more likely to do the same after release. Furthermore, it is reasoned that normalization helps facilitate inmate adjustment to the prison environment. By being held accountable, by being encouraged to act responsibly, and by preparing for their future release, inmates find structure and direction that has often been lacking. It goes without saying that proper facility adjustment is a precursor to proper social adjustment. In essence, if an offender can properly assimilate into the prison culture and adapt to the expectations of its officials, he/she will be better prepared to reenter society upon release. To this end, psychological, educational, vocational, and drug treatment programs are liberally offered. This approach also values constitutional and human rights protections. Thus, under this approach few impediments exist to inmates filing institutional grievances or seeking redress through the judiciary. Judicial access has long signified an open style of management where each inmate is valued and considered worthy of both the government's consideration and its protection.

As stated, under normalization inmates are given a great degree of control over their daily activities. To this end, normalization employs an open and participatory style of management. This approach encourages inmates to become actively involved in the operation of the prison itself. This often involves the solicitation of inmate input on nonsecurity issues and permits inmates to help design recreational and treatment activities. Through direct participation, inmates are taught responsibility and often become instrumental in the design of their own treatment programs. Participatory involvement of this nature increases the likelihood of a successful outcome. To illustrate this point, imagine a time in your life when you were told to do something. You may have resented such an order. In fact, you may have resisted it, even sabotaged the outcome. Had you been given even a small degree of control over your own actions, your reaction, and the subsequent outcome, might have been very different. Inmates are just like the rest of us. Often inmates will openly resist authority unless given some degree of control over their own actions. It is this control that tends to create positive perceptions related to an inmate's adherence to institutional rules as well as his/her participation in treatment programming. Positive perceptions are often produced by the manner in which people are approached. It is these perceptions that can significantly increase the chances for positive results. Participatory involvement is especially important when dealing with inmates who may resent having little or no control over their daily lives.

In an opposite fashion, under the ideology of **less eligibility** prison officials largely ignore inmates' rights and provide few amenities. Similarly, few opportunities are provided for inmates to participate in vocational, educational, or recreational programs. Instead, the prison serves as a human depository—a warehouse that specializes in storing felons. As such, little opportunity exists for inmates to engage in constructive or creative activities. Less eligibility also stresses operations that are efficient and private. Efficiency dictates the removal of all but those necessities required to sustain life. Since privacy is also valued, intervention by the judiciary into what may be perceived as "internal matters" is discouraged. Instead, inmates are encouraged and perhaps even required to route complaints through internal grievance processes. Since this approach values efficiency, privacy, and isolation from the judiciary, concerns persist about abuse. Opponents of this approach often state that isolation has historically been a precursor to many forms of human rights atrocities. Prisons operating under this management style have often been described by inmates as being more dehumanizing and isolating than those prisons operating under normalization. In fact, inmates generally refer to management practices that adhere to normalization as being "open" in nature while describing less eligibility as being "closed." Of course, an open system values operational transparency. More will be said about operational transparency later, but transparency suggests that management approaches are more likely to be fair and consistent, and to adhere to constitutional standards.

By now, you should have gathered from this presentation that there is a growing debate about the overall purpose of the prison and about its management practices. To understand the contemporary prison and its operations more fully, we must consider those objectives that have traditionally influenced its actions.

Correctional Objectives

Before proceeding, it is necessary to recognize that a great deal of uncertainty surrounds the operation of the modern prison. This becomes evident when reviewing prison-related literature, most of which fails to identify the historical and contemporary objectives of this institution. Of that literature that does identify the prison's operational objectives, most ignores inmate reform as a legitimate penal pursuit. Instead, the prison is often portrayed as little more than a temporary holding tank for society's offenders. This avoidance of identifying the numerous objectives of the prison is the direct result of a confusion that currently permeates both the institution and the correctional profession. The reason this confusion exists is not readily evident; however, the prison system has recently experienced a gargantuan influx of inmates. This influx has resulted in severe overcrowding. Overcrowding, in turn, has necessitated the adoption of a rigid form of institutional security, the likes of which has never before been seen. It is in the midst of this massive influx of offenders and the need for strict control over dangerously large inmate populations that officials have become confused about the prison's purpose and place in modern society. Furthermore, overcrowding requires that treatment programs be cut in order to reduce operating expenditures. After all, a tripling of the inmate population over the past 15 years requires that prison officials reduce spending on all but the basic necessities. Education, vocational training, and counseling programs have all been drastically cut. Overcrowding and a reduction in rehabilitative programming have led to an operational approach called "no-frills incarceration." **No-frills incarceration** refers to reducing or eliminating those amenities and treatment programs that are not operationally essential. This approach holds that the only worthwhile objective of the prison is the temporary containment of the offender. Of course, this has resulted in an inmate population that is bored, hopeless, and largely unprepared for release. Such an approach is truly unfortunate, since in the absence of a firm grounding in traditional penal objectives, the prison will increasingly find itself at odds with both its historical mandates and societal interests. Let us review the traditional objectives of the prison. This review fills a recognizable void in the literature. This is especially significant in an age when no-frills incarceration is undertaken without a clear understanding of its long-term effect on either the inmate or society. What are these traditional objectives? They are generally identified as institutional security, rehabilitation, retribution/punishment, incapacitation, and deterrence. Let us begin our review with institutional security.

Institutional Security

It should come as no great surprise that prisons are specifically designed to be secure institutions. Security requires absolute control over the movement of all persons and objects into and out of these facilities. To ensure that prisons remain secure, they rely upon specially trained personnel and structural barriers. Let us begin our review of institutional security by considering security personnel. Security personnel are commonly called guards or correctional officers. These individuals are typically uniformed and hold military-style rank. These rank range from correctional officer (the entry-level position) to sergeant, lieutenant, captain, and major. Members of each rank report directly to those individuals holding the next highest rank. This is referred to as the **chain of**

command. For example, a correctional officer reports to a sergeant, and a sergeant reports to a lieutenant. **Correctional officers** regardless of rank have been given the strict mandate to maintain a safe and secure institution. To do this, correctional officers conduct scheduled and random inmate counts, ensure inmates are at their designated locations, enforce institutional rules, supervise inmate activities, and patrol the internal and external areas of the institution.

Prisons also use a number of **structural barriers** to ensure that security is maintained. The purpose of the structural barrier is to enhance institutional safety by making unauthorized movement difficult or impossible. Through control of inmate movement, the likelihood of violent acts and escapes is reduced. Structural barriers include doors, walls, fences, various alarm systems, and concertina wire. **Concertina wire** (also referred to as **razor wire**) uses razors instead of the barbs that are found on common agricultural fencing. These razors are finely honed and can easily penetrate clothing and flesh. Originally developed for military use, concertina wire is often deployed in large rolls. When deployed in this fashion, it is secured to the tops of walls or fences or even arranged in pyramid fashion. When used in **pyramid fashion,** two or more rolls are deployed along the base of a wall or fence, with additional rolls stacked atop. This makes it virtually impossible for inmates to get close enough to scale a wall or fence.

Institutional security specifically seeks to

- prevent escape,
- prevent violence,
- control unauthorized inmate movement, and
- ensure a safe environment for inmates, employees, and visitors.

When security fails its mandate not only do prisons become unsafe, but it becomes impossible for them to operate effectively. When a particular prison becomes too dangerous, staff may abandon it by transferring to a safer facility or by using large amounts of vacation and sick leave. As you can imagine, both of these activities further destabilize an unsafe institution. Similarly, if a prison is unsafe, inmates may resort to self-protection by carrying crudely fashioned weapons called shivs or shanks. A **shiv** or **shank** is a weapon that resembles an ice pick or knife. Often this type of weapon is fashioned from a piece of steel, tightly rolled newspaper, or more commonly a comb or toothbrush. A weapon of this nature is designed to cut or stab. The presence of any type of weapon in a correctional institution further undermines security efforts. Institutional security is the basis upon which all facility operations and objectives depend. Without an effective security apparatus, no other objective can be achieved.

Rehabilitation

Inmate reform is both a personal and a social victory

As its objective, **rehabilitation** attempts to instill within the inmate self-respect, respect for others, and in particular a respect for the law. The ultimate goal of rehabilitation is to produce a socially responsible and law-abiding citizen. Admittedly, this is a difficult task, since few offenders have been properly socialized and even fewer possess the skills, education, or training needed to obtain and maintain gainful employment. The ability of an ex-inmate to make a living beyond mere subsistence is often considered the key to personal reform and social reintegration. Many citizens expect the prison to equip the offender with the skills necessary to assure a law-abiding lifestyle upon release. Gainful employment not only provides a source of income but also effectively channels an ex-inmate's attention toward a productive activity—leaving little time or energy for less positive endeavors. Without adequate preparation for postrelease employment, offenders frequently find themselves reverting to old habits and self-destructive behaviors. Rehabilitation seeks to prevent this and is based upon the following beliefs:

- people can change,
- offenders and nonoffenders are similar (especially in their motivations and desires),
- offenders exercise free will based in part on available opportunities,
- many offenders do not have the skills or education necessary to obtain gainful employment,
- education and vocational training provide the knowledge and skills necessary for gainful employment,
- treatment and counseling help offenders confront and conquer self-destructive behaviors,

- rehabilitation is a process that is most effective when based upon free and open participation, and
- reform will occur only through a system that recognizes and values it.

As you may have surmised, the ultimate goal of rehabilitation is the reformation and long-term success of the inmate. Success is usually defined as the ability of the ex-inmate to lead a law-abiding lifestyle upon release. Success in this endeavor benefits society in terms of reduced crime rates, healthier communities, and reductions in correctional expenditures. Thus, it can be said that a rehabilitative ideology is forward-looking since it proactively seeks to improve both the individual and society. Inmate reform initiatives seek to create a prison experience that is both meaningful and productive. Time, which is the most abundant resource available to both the inmate and prison official, can be used to prepare each inmate for a postrelease crime-free life. To understand rehabilitation better, it is necessary to consider the role that rehabilitation has traditionally played in European and American prisons.

> *What if . . . prison officials were to again stress a rehabilitative approach to prison operations? Would the prison's social value and prestige increase?*

As early as the sixteenth century, prison operators recognized the value of offender reform. Prisons at this time were attempting to reduce criminality through inmate reform. These early institutions sought to produce a productive citizenry by providing inmates with work-related skills. It was believed that through education and skill development, employment and a law-abiding lifestyle would naturally ensue. At one time or another all prisons to varying degrees sought offender reform through isolation, corrective discipline, hard labor, or intense religious indoctrination. While we may now disapprove of some of these techniques, the purpose behind them was altruistic in nature.

Colonial America also embraced a reform ideology. Colonists demanded that criminal sanctions stress rehabilitation. A reform ideology was based largely upon Christian principles. These early communities believed in the value of humanity, repentance, and the ultimate salvation of the offender. This approach is reflected in the use of sanctions that were more lenient than those used in other nations. For example, the Massachusetts and Pennsylvania colonies preferred imprisonment for their offenders to the more brutal corporal and capital punishments prescribed under traditional English law. This suggests that colonists valued humanitarian forms of treatment and recognized the reformative powers of imprisonment—had they not, they would have chosen other actions that could have been administered more quickly and cheaply. The emphasis on a reform ideology is thoroughly detailed in **William Paley's** *Principles of Moral and Political Philosophy* (1785). Although Paley (1743–1805) was an English philosopher and religious leader, his works were widely known and read by colonists. Paley wrote extensively on the subjects of free will, right and wrong, repentance, and the role that each plays in one's redemption. Paley's book not only helped establish the principles of the early American prison system but also cemented rehabilitation as the principal objective of the early colonial prison. Furthermore, in 1787 a group of colonial leaders met at the home of **Benjamin Franklin,** where they officially endorsed rehabilitation as a penal pursuit. Inmate reform was aggressively pursued without challenge for the next 100 years. Then, at the 1870 meeting of the **National Prison Association** (now the American Correctional Association) penologists reaffirmed the importance of inmate reform. This ensured that inmate reform would be a pursuit of the prison for another 100 years. The identification and pursuit of rehabilitation as a goal of the early prison clearly reveals the value placed upon it by prison officials and the general citizenry.

While the history of rehabilitation is easily chronicled on both a national and an international basis, inmate reform as a penal pursuit finds little contemporary support among practitioners and scholars alike. The beginning of rehabilitation's decline, especially among our nation's top scholars, can be traced to the 1970s, when criminal justice researchers began to pronounce inmate reform to be unobtainable. The more noteworthy of these individuals include **Robert Martinson** and his "nothing works" report, **James Q. Wilson** and his *Thinking about Crime*, and **David Fogel** and his *We Are the Living Proof: The Justice Model of Corrections.* Each of these academicians challenged inmate reform as a practice and penal ideology. These individuals consistently identified numerous factors associated with the prison's seeming inability to reform large numbers of inmates. These factors included overcrowding, the expense of reform initiatives, and the lack of cooperation and interest among the inmate population. The antireform attack launched by these scholars coupled with rising crime rates and the subsequent growth in our prison population was used by opponents of rehabilitation to attack and further weaken those programs that were already in existence.

It was around this time that two major prison riots occurred that captured the attention of national and international observers. The first of these occurred in 1971 at the **Attica Correctional Facility** located in upstate New York. During this riot, 43 individuals were killed (11 of whom were staff). Many of those killed lost their lives during the poorly planned and initiated "retaking" of the institution. The scenes of this horrific event burned an image of the contemporary offender into the minds of the citizenry that is still very much alive today. When I ask my students to visualize a prison riot, they often mention the one that occurred at Attica. Then, in February 1980, a riot occurred at the Penitentiary of New Mexico. Again, scenes of extreme cruelty and uncontrolled chaos were broadcast worldwide. Average citizens were horrified at the scenes being transmitted into their living rooms. Images of a burning prison surrounded by heavily armed Guardsmen and reports of widespread murder, torture, and rape captured a nation's attention. It was estimated that about 150 inmates actively participated in this event. After 36 hours, the prison was retaken without incident. In its aftermath, it was discovered that 33 inmates had been killed, with untold others having been attacked and injured. Inmate leadership behind both of these riots claimed that overcrowding, poor living conditions, and a refusal by prison administrations to address inmate concerns were contributory factors for these events. Generally, penologists define a **riot** as a collective action that constitutes a forcible attempt to gain control of an entire correctional institution or some part thereof. By controlling an institution, inmates hope to negotiate for improved living conditions or changes to a prison's operational procedures. In comparison, **inmate disturbances** are much smaller in scale and involve inmates who have no desire to gain control of an institution or to force sweeping change. Instead these inmates often choose to participate in simple acts of institutional disobedience. The dynamics of prison riots has contributed to what has become known as the **Environmental Theory of Prison Violence.** This perspective suggests that prison conditions are a leading factor in most inmate uprisings. These insurrections are often seen by the inmate population as the only avenue available to air grievances and improve conditions. While entire books have been written on riots and their subsequent effect upon prison operations, to all intents and purposes the Attica and Santa Fe riots

- introduced the average citizen to the prison,
- highlighted a violent but atypical event,
- were accepted by many as representative of typical inmate behavior,
- were sensationalized by journalists, who portrayed inmates as being in need of increased discipline and control, and
- caused supporters of inmate reform to question rehabilitative ideology, further weakening reform initiatives.

The Attica and Santa Fe riots helped solidify the movement already underway that claimed inmate reform to be an unachievable and outdated objective. Support for this sentiment grew during the decade following Santa Fe, due, in part, to the most violent and turbulent ten-year period ever experienced by the American prison. Participants in this movement claimed that the best approach to dealing with the modern inmate was through control and containment. It was believed that through isolation and strict control over the actions and movements of the inmate population, events similar to Attica and Santa Fe would never reoccur.

Generally, scholars concur that financial factors are the biggest obstacle that must be overcome in order to achieve inmate reform. At a time when prison populations are large, available funds are being used to meet the many necessities of maintaining massive inmate populations. Fulfilling these needs often leaves little if any funding for "discretionary" programming. Admittedly, from a financial perspective, reform initiatives are costly. Of all the objectives of the prison, rehabilitation is by far the most expensive to achieve. Opponents of inmate reform claim that

- reform is more expensive than simple incarceration and requires large outlays of time and resources,
- it is difficult to locate and retain qualified staff willing to work in a secure environment for modest compensation,
- reform ideology runs contrary to conservative expectations of a harsh and punitive penal system, and
- reform requires inmate cooperation with treatment initiatives, but many offenders are unwilling to participate in rehabilitative programming.

It is primarily due to overcrowding, a shortage of available funding, a desire to "get tough" on crime, and a changing concept of the inmate that reform ideology has steadily lost support. No one particular event or factor is responsible for this occurrence. Instead, all have taken their toll on the way we perceive and approach inmate reform. Declining support for rehabilitation has effectively freed the prison from the traditional expectation that it reform the offender. Instead, the prison is becoming much more **internally oriented**. An internal orientation suggests that prison administrators increasingly measure success not in terms of recidivism, which was the traditional measure of a prison's success, but through measures of various internal attributes. These internal attributes include operating budgets (the lower the better), the number of inmates a facility can hold (the more the better), and the number of days since a prison last experienced a violent act or an escape. This shift is significant since it enables prison officials to focus exclusively upon those measures that reflect positively on their performance. Furthermore, an internal orientation allows operators to emphasize those correctional objectives that are easily realized. One objective that is commonly associated with the prison and is easily achieved is the production of pain and discomfort. Let us now turn our attention toward the role played by retribution and punishment in prison operations.

Retribution/Punishment

Revenge is the prison's most primitive objective

Retribution is characterized by the phrase "an eye for an eye." Retribution is little more than retaliation or revenge against those who harm us. Retribution and punishment seek to inflict pain upon the offender. However, unlike retribution, punishment inflicts pain to correct improper behavior. In this sense, punishment can be an instructional tool similar to the type of activity a parent might engage in to teach a child proper behavior. While the motivations behind these objectives differ slightly, the recipient may perceive little or no difference. Historically, retribution and punishment were administered by the victim of a crime or by his/her family. Retribution and punishment were often a private matter since few authorities were willing to pursue, apprehend, and punish the law violator. As society became more complex, government officials assumed the responsibility of dealing with the criminal. Once this process began, retribution and the nongovernmental application of punishment were outlawed.

While the prison does not sanction or endorse retribution, imprisonment is a form of punishment. Imprisonment is a form of punishment because it

- deprives an inmate of his/her freedoms, autonomy, and access to goods and services,
- relegates each inmate to a low standard of living, and
- isolates the inmate from his/her community, family, and loved ones.

Both retribution and punishment traditionally have asserted that for every injury caused by a crime, a prescribed injury must in turn be administered to the offending party. In modern society, legal jurisprudence prohibits injury through physical means. Therefore, this "prescribed injury" within the contemporary context really means the loss of freedom and the social isolation that result from imprisonment. Punishment seeks to

- inflict pain and injury on those who break the law,
- express social disapproval for illegal behavior,
- correct improper or unacceptable behavior, and
- produce a deterrent effect.

A natural byproduct of punishment is deterrence. Deterrence is based upon the **pleasure–pain principle**. This principle suggests that offenders will learn to avoid criminal acts if those acts typically result in pain. Let us now consider deterrence as a penal objective.

Deterrence

Deterrence seeks to convince offenders and "would-be" offenders that conformity is in their best interests

Deterrence ideology seeks to convince offenders and "would-be" offenders that criminal acts will result in punishment. Therefore, criminal acts should be avoided. Penologists recognize two types of deterrence. The first is specific deterrence and occurs at the individual level. Here, the punishment that someone is subjected to is intended to dissuade him/her from committing additional crimes. This approach is based upon the concept of hedonism. **Hedonism,** or the pleasure–pain principle, suggests that individuals generally conduct a cost-to-benefit analysis with regard to their actions. Thus, if a past punishment was especially painful, an offender will likely avoid similar acts in the future.

The second type of deterrence is general deterrence. General deterrence is much broader in scope than specific deterrence since it seeks to convince potential criminals that the pains associated with crime outweigh the benefits. The punishment of individual offenders discourages others from acting in a similar fashion. Thus, when an individual offender is punished, his/her punishment serves as an example of what may happen to others should they commit similar acts. To better understand general deterrence let us consider deterrence from a business perspective. In much the same way a businessperson determines what transactions are profitable, potential criminals calculate the benefits of their actions against the potential losses. The basis for this calculation will always be the punishment that is typically associated with the act being considered, and the only way to get this information is by considering the punishments that others have experienced. Much like the businessperson, a potential offender will avoid those actions that might result in loss or pain. The primary difference between specific and general deterrence is in the number of people each seeks to influence. Specific deterrence seeks to influence individuals already convicted of a crime, whereas general deterrence seeks to influence those who are contemplating the commission of a crime. General deterrence is often used as the basis for supporting the televising of executions. Proponents of this approach suggest that televising executions will deter others from criminal activity.

Incapacitation/Banishment

Incapacitation and banishment are functional equivalents—both remove the offender from society

Banishment is an age-old practice. It seeks to separate the offender from society. We see this practice in early cultures where those individuals who grievously or habitually broke established customs were expelled from the family or tribe. Expulsion benefited society by

- preventing further predation,
- limiting an offender's ability to corrupt others, and
- serving as a general deterrent.

Banishment was an especially feared sanction because it often resulted in death. Without the protection and assistance of the group, banished offenders found it difficult to acquire shelter, clothing, and food. Imagine the hardships that were encountered in trying to meet one's most basic needs. As societies grew and became more complex, they eventually formed countries. Countries also used banishment as a criminal sanction. For example, England banished many of its offenders to North America. Yes, many of America's earliest citizens were criminals sent here from England! Over 30,000 offenders were sent to the American colonies. Australia shares this heritage. Even the French banished offenders to such remote locations as Madagascar and New Caledonia. More recently, Russia (until 1990) banished offenders to the desolate regions of Siberia. While it is no longer conceivable to banish offenders to sparsely populated areas of the world, banishment has been given a contemporary spin. Offenders are still banished, but they are banished to the prison, where they are incapacitated. Current practices amount to little more than institutional banishment. This practice effectively removes the offender from society while expressing little interest in his/her reform or well-being.

Incapacitation is currently a popular practice. In 1980, almost half of those individuals convicted in federal court received a prison sentence; by 2001, this number had increased to about 75 percent. A similar trend is also observable at the state level. Not only are offenders being imprisoned more frequently, but sentence length is also increasing. Sentence lengths have doubled and even tripled for many felony offenses. Get-tough legislation like "three strikes and you're out" has significantly increased both incarceration rates and sentence length for a large portion of the offender population. This has helped produce a large prison population. In 1980, there were about 300,000 inmates in the nation's prison system. Current figures suggest that we now have in excess of 2 million incarcerated individuals. The increased use of incarceration and increases in sentence length indicate a growing movement toward removing greater percentages of offenders from society. While banishment and incapacitation are quite similar in many respects, the most significant difference between the two is that most contemporary offenders will eventually return to society.

Observations

There is little doubt that the contemporary prison employee is better educated and trained than was his/her predecessor. It is increasingly common to find prison staff with college degrees and professional certifications. Furthermore, the **American Correctional Association** (the nation's foremost body of prison/correctional employees) has helped standardize and improve training curricula. Following the riot of 1980, officials at the Penitentiary of New Mexico also recognized the importance of employee training. Officials set about creating a state-of-the-art training academy. In 1993, the New Mexico Correctional Training Academy earned the distinction of being the first academy to be awarded accreditation by the American Correctional Association. This $11 million academy trains more than 1,200 staff each year and has become an example for academies nationwide. Accreditation by this association is now the standard in the profession.

Despite increased education and training, many prison employees remain uncertain about the prison's purpose or role within society. Colleges have done little to remedy this situation. Few colleges provide prison-related courses, opting instead to focus curricula on the more "glamorous and exciting" field of law enforcement. To find a college or university offering comprehensive courses on the prison is rare. Collectively, few training academies and college programs consistently teach students the history or traditional objectives of the prison. I am personally familiar with numerous academies and college programs nationwide and none to my knowledge devotes adequate time or attention to these subjects. Even in training courses for supervisory prison personnel, I have yet to hear any mention of the prison's traditional goals. Instead, what is mentioned are financial considerations as well as security. This is unfortunate since it permits the prison to

- operate without an awareness of its history,
- operate with few ideological underpinnings, and
- operate with few, if any, long-term strategies related to the promotion of public safety.

Without a recognized link to its past, the prison is increasingly retreating into a self-created world where it is protected from outside challenge. Here, it is free to operate with little interference. This permits officials to manage prisons in a manner that downplays the importance of civil rights protections while embracing the tenets of less eligibility. This isolation has led to a decrease in the prison's ability to promote public safety. Concerned citizens as well as penologists increasingly recognize that our prisons are failing to promote the public's long-term interests. To promote community safety more effectively, it is essential that employees become familiar with the prison's history and traditional objectives and that officials recognize the importance of inmate reform within the larger realm of public safety. The sooner officials admit that the prison is not living up to its historical mandates or contemporary obligations, the sooner change will take place. An awareness of the prison's history and objectives is essential if we are to address the prison's many short-comings. Therefore, practitioners, scholars, and progressive public leaders must all demand that prison employees be introduced to the prison's guiding principles, history, and how both relate to the contemporary correctional setting. It is only through such an approach that inmate reform will be recognized as an essential element in the prison's overall mission to promote the public's long-term safety.

Summary

Penologists generally recognize that traditional ideologies, especially as they relate to inmate reform, are being ignored by today's prison officials. Instead a conservative political climate and financial constraints have promoted an operational approach that values inmate control and containment. Few amenities and comforts now exist to help mitigate the harsh penal environment. Furthermore, few opportunities now exist for inmates to become involved in productive pursuits designed specifically to prepare them for postrelease life. Penologists are increasingly referring to this approach as "no-frills incarceration." Without the ability to pursue education or develop or maintain a skill during incarceration, many inmates are returning to society angry, unemployable, and poorly suited for social readjustment.

Even though the prison now seeks to control inmate populations to a greater degree than ever before, it is unable to escape its own history—a history that is steeped in a tradition of inmate reform. While such a history exists, the contemporary prison employee is unfamiliar with this history, the traditional objectives of the prison, or how these objectives translate into modern practice. A workforce that is unaware of its history and traditional objectives is a workforce that is not guided by a sense of professionalism or vision. However, there remains awareness among some practitioners and penologists that the prison should do more than temporarily isolate the offender. These individuals recognize that it is only through inmate reform that society can be made safer. In the next chapter, we will take a closer look at characteristics of the contemporary inmate and prison.

Chapter Highlights

1. Penology is the study of the prison, its objectives, and those whom it employs and incarcerates.
2. At the center of penology is an interest in inmate treatment.
3. Prison operations currently emphasize efficiency and inmate containment.
4. There are two philosophies of prison operations—normalization and less eligibility.
5. Under the philosophy of normalization, inmates are given considerable freedom and are encouraged to make responsible decisions.
6. Under the philosophy of less eligibility, inmate rights are largely ignored and few amenities are provided.

7. The traditional goals of the prison include institutional security, reha-bilitation, retribution, deterrence, and incapacitation.

8. Institutional security must exist before any other objective can be pursued.

9. Rehabilitation attempts to instill within the offender a respect for him-self/herself, others, and particularly the law.

10. The ultimate goal of rehabilitation is to produce a socially responsible and law-abiding citizen.

11. A rehabilitative rationale seeks to create a prison experience that is productive and meaningful.

12. Rehabilitation is no longer an aggressively pursued objective of the prison.

13. Generally, scholars agree that financial factors are the leading obstacle to inmate reform.

14. Retribution is summarized in the phrase "an eye for an eye."

15. Punishment is the prison's most primitive objective. It seeks to inflict pain on the offender.

16. Deterrence attempts to dissuade violators and potential violators from committing crimes.

17. Banishment is an age-old practice that seeks to separate the offender from society.

18. Banishment was an especially feared sanction because it often resulted in death.

19. Incapacitation, much like banishment, removes the offender from society.

20. The prison experiences difficulty in attracting and retaining educated and professionally oriented employees.

21. Generally, while today's correctional employee is better educated and trained than his/her predecessor, he/she remains unaware of the prison's history or traditional objectives.

22. A workforce that is not aware of its own history is a workforce that is not guided by a sense of professionalism or vision.

Discussion Questions

1. How accurate is the statement "Many changes in society affect the lowest strata first"? In your response, consider how changes in the prison may signal forthcoming changes in other areas of society.

2. What are the traditional objectives of the prison? Which objective has lost support among prison operators? Which, in your opinion, is now the dominant goal?

3. Is it proper to make comparisons between incapacitation and banish-ment? What are the similarities and differences?

4. How can penology help improve the contemporary prison?
5. Why does the prison find difficulty in attracting and retaining educated and professionally oriented employees?
6. Are inmates treated too harshly or too leniently by the prison? In your opinion, how should inmates be treated? What advantages does your suggestion provide?
7. In your opinion, is inmate reform a legitimate penal pursuit? Why or why not?
8. In what ways are offenders and nonoffenders similar? In what ways are they different? Explain.

Sources

Blakely, C. 2005. *America's Prisons: The Movement toward Profit and Privatization*. Florida: Brown Walker Press.

Earley, P. 1993. *The Hot House: Life inside Leavenworth Prison*. New York: Bantam Books.

Fogel, D. 1975. *We Are the Living Proof: The Justice Model for Corrections*. Cincinnati: Anderson.

James, H. B., and J. Bruton. 2004. *The Big House: Life inside a Supermax Security Prison*. Minnesota: Voyageur Press.

James, Q. W. 1985. *Thinking about Crime*. London: Vintage.

Paley, W. 1785. *The Principles of Moral and Political Philosophy*. Indianapolis: Liberty Fund.

Roger, M. 1988. *The Devil's Butcher Shop: The New Mexico Prison Uprising*. Albuquerque: University of New Mexico Press.

Wayne, K. P., and B. L. Alt. 1997. *Slaughter in Cell House 3—The Anatomy of a Riot*. vanderGeest Publishing.

To consider the prison is to consider the inmate. It is the relationship that exists between the two that is the defining feature of each.

Chapter Two

Inmates and Incapacitation

To obtain a better understanding of the prison one must first become familiar with the inmate. To consider the prison apart from the inmate would be to ignore the very essence of the institution. You cannot separate the prison from the inmate, nor can you separate the inmate from the prison. It is the relationship that exists between the two that is the defining feature of each.

Before proceeding, it is imperative to recognize that there exists in any group, regardless of how diverse that group may be, a strong probability that its members share a number of characteristics. Observant visitors to any prison will quickly recognize commonalties in its inmate population. Not only do shared traits exist among the inmate population of any particular institution (**intra-prison commonalties**) but commonalties also exist among inmates nationwide (**inter-prison commonalties**). These traits make it possible for us to speak about the "average" or "typical" inmate. Of course, the value in speaking of the typical inmate is that it enables us to acquire a better understanding of those factors that appear to be correlated with criminality and, more important, the types of prison operations and interventions that they require.

The Contemporary Inmate

Contrary to popular belief, there are no physical differences
between the offender and nonoffender

To those who have never visited a prison as part of a field trip or perhaps
a community tour, let me offer assurance that inmates look no different
than the rest of us. They can be tall, short, fat, thin, and handsome as well
as downright repulsive. Some are old and others are young. Yet no
physical characteristic distinguishes them from the nonoffender.
Oftentimes, people assume that criminals are especially grotesque or
unappealing; after all, villains are often depicted as ugly or monster-like
by popular culture. This is a direct result of a long criminological history
that attempts to link physical traits with criminal behavior. Remember
Cesare Lombroso (1836–1909)? Lombroso, a nineteenth-century Italian
army physician, coined the rather unflattering term "atavism." This term
suggests that the criminal is a throwback to primitive humankind. After
studying the bodies of hundreds of criminals, Lombroso concluded that
offenders were primitive in nature and, therefore, incapable of coping with
the complexities of modern society. Unable to cope, many atavists had
little alternative but to resort to crime. In fact, the field of **criminal anthro-
pology** began as the study of the relationship between physical characteristics and criminal behavior. The earlier work of **Franz Gall** (1758–1828),
a German physiologist, linked the shape of one's skull to the development
of the underlying brain. If the skull appeared misformed or primitive in
nature, then it stood to reason that the underlying brain must be primitive as well. The study of the size and shape of the skull and its role in
criminal behavior is known as **phrenology**. These approaches, when
combined with **Charles Darwin's** (1809–1882) theory of evolution, con-
vinced many that the criminal was little more than the contemporary
equivalent—both physically and mentally—of a caveman. Physical traits
that have been studied for their possible connection to criminality include
the following:

- hair—length, color, and thickness,
- eye shape and coloration,
- nose shape,

- forehead size and shape,
- tooth size, shape, and decay,
- protrusion of the jaw,
- chin size and shape,
- ear size and shape,
- facial asymmetry, and
- body size and shape.

It is those characteristics that we associate with the popular image of "primitive humans" that have traditionally been believed to be correlates of criminality. For example, it was expected that individuals with thick hair growth, long flat noses, and pronounced eyebrow ridges were more primitive than others without such features. Early depictions of the offender portrayed him/her as "beast-like." It was surmised that if the body was primitive, so too was the intellect. A recent television commercial humorously depicts this belief. In it, a producer has inadvertently insulted a group of modern cavemen. The producer states, "It's so easy, even a caveman can do it." After he becomes aware that he has insulted some of his own employees as well as the viewing public, he attempts to make amends by taking a few cavemen out for supper at a posh restaurant. Of course, these cavemen are dressed nicely and act quite sophisticated—just the opposite of what is expected. The producer then apologizes and admits that he is surprised that cave people still exist. This prompts one caveman to suggest to the producer that he conduct appropriate research before making insensitive statements of this nature in the future. This commercial is entertaining because it depicts the primitive man as having the intellectual abilities and sensitivities of the modern human. While these commercial cavemen are quite different from popular depictions, "the offender as primitive man" has long been portrayed as being easily distinguishable from the nonoffender. Of course, such a belief is absolutely absurd! The criminal is physically indistinguishable from the noncriminal, and the intellectual abilities of each are similar. Not only are we physically and intellectually similar, but we also have many of the same aspirations. In fact, were you given several hours to speak with a group of inmates you would undoubtedly discover many shared experiences and interests. While there are no physical traits that distinguish offenders from the general population, inmates as a group do tend to share a number of characteristics (race, gender, and age) that deserve further mention.

The following tables provide data about the prison and the contemporary inmate. Information, including race, gender, age at the time of admission, the security level at which inmates are held, as well as the average number of months of incarceration, is provided for both the public and private sectors. The subject of the private prison is dealt with in much greater detail in chapter 4; for now it is enough to know that the private sector is becoming increasingly involved in prison operations. The private sector's involvement in corrections helps meet the insatiable need for prison space, thereby fortifying government operations.

Table 2.1 reveals that federal and private correctional authorities have both expanded operations via additional prisons. The greatest increase in new prisons is in the private sector. The private sector added 72 new prisons over the nine-year period considered. Surprisingly, figures suggest that states have reduced the total number of facilities they operate. While initially appearing improbable, a reduction in the number of state-operated facilities is due to the increased reliance upon the private sector to assume operations of existing prisons as well as to build facilities to house inmate overflow. **Inmate overflow** is that portion of the inmate population that cannot safely be housed in existing, overcrowded public prisons. Furthermore, states are expanding their preexisting prisons rather than break ground on new construction. This approach provides additional space quickly and without large financial outlays. The total number of inmates held in federal, state, and private prisons also increased substantially. The trend depicted in table 2.1 is expected to continue well into the future, suggesting further expansion of private sector operations and continuing increases in incarceration rates.

A review of table 2.2 reveals that a disproportionate number of offenders are African American. **African Americans** make up roughly 12 percent of the American population but account for about 45 percent of the inmate population. Questions about this overrepresentation persist. While numerous explanations have been offered to explain this figure, research largely discredits popular claims of a racist and discriminatory criminal justice system. Instead, more recent explanations focus upon family structure, education, employment, economics, and

TABLE 2.1. Number of Facilities and Inmates by Jurisdiction

	1995	2004	Change
Number of facilities			
Federal	75	84	+9
State	1,056	1,023	−33
Private	29	101	+72
Number of inmates			
Federal	89,538	169,370	+79,832
State	989,004	1,241,034	+252,030
Private	18,294	98,791	+80,497

Sources: Stephan and Karberg, 2003; Harrison and Beck, 2005.
Note: Information based upon most current data available and estimates.

TABLE 2.2. Demographic and Prison Custody Level Data

Characteristic	Public	Private	Average
Inmates			
Race			
Black (%)	47	43	45
White (%)	43	32	38
Other/unknown (%)	9	25	17
Gender			
Male (%)	94	90	92
Female (%)	6	10	8
Age at admission (years)	31	30	31
49 or less (%)	93	94	93
50 or older (%)	7	6	7
Average sentence served			
by inmates (months)	28	11	20
Prisons			
Custody levels*			
Maximum (%)	27	6	16
Medium (%)	37	43	40
Minimum (%)	32	47	40
Capacity (%)	113	82	98

Sources: Stephan and Karberg, 2003; Criminal Justice Institute, 2000.
* Prison custody levels total 96 percent due to the exclusion of small facilities.

socialization as contributory factors. Furthermore, males make up about 48 percent of the general population but account for approximately 92 percent of the inmate population. Again, numerous explanations have been offered for this overrepresentation. Currently, most explanations focus on socialization processes and opportunity. Fewer consider biological factors such as testosterone and its relationship to aggression.

TABLE 2.3. Security Levels of Federal, State, and Private Prisons (No. of Prisons)

	Federal	State	Private	Total
Maximum	11	317	4	332
Medium	29	428	65	522
Minimum	44	575	195	814

Source: U.S. Department of Justice, Bureau of Justice Statistics, 2003.

Not only is the typical offender black and male but he is young as well. The average offender is only 30 years of age when imprisoned. Furthermore, the average term of incarceration is less than two years. Therefore, the "typical" inmate tends to be

- African American,
- male,
- young—just 30 years of age when confined—and
- convicted of nonserious offenses for which he will serve less than two years confinement.

Since most prisoners are young and male, they are often believed to be aggressive and violent. However, when considering the custody level at which many of these inmates are held, we discover that about 40 percent are incarcerated in minimum-security prisons. More will be said about prison security in the next section, but minimum-security prisons are reserved for inmates who pose little risk to society. This clearly reveals that many of today's offenders have been convicted of nonviolent, relatively nonserious offenses and show little or no proclivity toward violence (table 2.3).

Types of Prisons

Having briefly reviewed a few of the general characteristics of the contemporary inmate, let us now consider in greater detail the various types of prisons operating in the United States. Let us begin by considering the type of prison with the highest level of security available—a specialized prison commonly referred to as the supermax.

Supermax prisons represent the highest level of institutional security ever developed. Inmates who are confined in supermax prisons are often described as "the worst of the worst" or "super-predators." In a U.S. Department of Justice study, the supermax prison was described as follows:

> A freestanding facility, or a distinct unit within a freestanding facility, that provides for the management and secure control of inmates who have been officially designated as exhibiting violent or seriously disruptive behavior while incarcerated. Such inmates have been determined to be a threat to safety and security in traditional high-security facilities and their behavior can be controlled only by separation, restricted movement, and limited access to staff and other inmates. (Riveland, 1999)

Supermax prisons are specifically designed to house violent inmates who cannot safely be confined in lower-security institutions. Supermax inmates are considered a threat to staff and inmates alike. In fact, many have seriously injured or killed others while incarcerated. Still others have been identified as gang leaders who if left in lower-security prisons would threaten to destabilize institutional operations. To deal effectively with these individuals, supermax prisons totally confine and control their inmate populations. Often, incarceration in a supermax prison is described as little more than solitary confinement. **Solitary confinement** refers to confining inmates to their single-occupancy cells 23 hours each day. The hour spent outside the cell is used for recreation and bathing. By keeping inmates within their cells, opportunities for conflict, attack, and escape are minimized. Inmates are even served meals in their cells. Lights within each cell remain continuously lit so that observation is effortless. No opportunity for work or educational activities exists. Inmates often keep themselves occupied reading, watching television, writing letters, or sleeping.

Most supermax inmates report their experience as unpleasant and cruel. Many also speak about losing touch with reality. However, all admit that the supermax effectively accomplishes its objectives of isolation and control. For example, inmates never have contact with one another. Furthermore, all contact that occurs between inmates and staff is highly controlled and takes place only after the inmate has been fully restrained. Usually, inmates' hands and feet are shackled when they leave their cells. Additional precautions often include the use of belly-chains to further immobilize the hands and arms. Movement within the prison, when it occurs, is strictly regimented, with each inmate commanding an escort of two or more officers. Visits with family and friends occur through safety glass and an internal speaker system. At some supermax prisons, visitation may be conducted via closed-circuit television, with the inmate remaining in his cell. A few examples of supermax prisons are listed:

- **Alcatraz:** Alcatraz was America's highest-security prison until its closure in 1963. Located on an island in the San Francisco Bay, it has served as the prototype for all contemporary supermax facilities. Among its most infamous inmates were Al "Scarface" Capone, "Machine Gun" Kelly, and Robert Stroud, "The Birdman of Alcatraz."
- **U.S. Penitentiary, Marion, IL:** This prison opened in 1963, the very year Alcatraz closed—no mere coincidence. Marion became the new Alcatraz. One of the better-known inmates held at Marion was Jack Henry Abbott, who wrote *In the Belly of the Beast* (1981)—a national best-seller. Within six weeks of being released from Marion, Abbott stabbed a man to death in Manhattan.
- **Wisconsin Secure Program Facility:** This is Wisconsin's highest-security prison and has served as a model for many state-run supermax prisons.
- **Ad Max, Florence, CO:** This facility opened in 1994. It is commonly referred to as the "Alcatraz of the Rockies" and may be the highest-security prison ever built.
- **Pelican Bay State Prison, CA:** This state-of-the-art prison opened in 1989 and is one of the most advanced state-run supermax facilities in the country. A few of its more infamous inmates have included Charles Manson and "Monster" Cody. Cody is a former "Crips" member and author of *Monster*, which chronicles street gang life.

Maximum-security prisons, much like the supermax, emphasize inmate control and incapacitation. High walls, concertina wire, and observation towers are pronounced architectural features. The operational characteristics of supermax and maximum-security prisons are similar in many respects. However, inmates in the maximum-security prison are permitted limited contact with one another. There may also be limited educational, employment, and recreational opportunities.

Quite often, maximum-security inmates were initially housed in lower-security facilities but proved unable or unwilling to abide by institutional rules. Many maximum-security inmates have shown a propensity toward violence but may not be as violent as their supermax counterparts. Maximum-security inmates are often high-ranking gang members. The purpose of the maximum-security prison is to control inmate movement and limit an inmate's ability to communicate with other inmates, especially when gang involvement is a concern. Quite often, maximum-security inmates are also confined to their cells for long durations. It is common to find supermax and maximum-security prisons combined to form one larger correctional compound.

Medium-security prisons impose fewer restrictions on inmate movement and interaction than do maximum-security prisons. There are also additional opportunities for inmates to participate in education, employment, and recreational pursuits. Inmates may be housed in single- or double-occupancy cells or in a dormitory-style setting. Physical contact is usually permitted between inmates and visitors but may be highly controlled and limited. Some medium-security prisons also permit conjugal visitation. **Conjugal visitation** allows inmates and their spouses to have sexual contact. Visits of this nature often take place in small apartment-style rooms that are completely furnished. These visits, usually lasting from two to eight hours, reward inmates who maintain clear conduct. An inmate establishes **clear conduct** when he abides by all institutional rules and regulations. Clear conduct is a prerequisite for participation in all conjugal visitation programs. In this manner, conjugal visitation privileges are a management tool that helps officials control the inmate population. Failure to abide by an institution's rules and regulations can result in a misconduct report. A **misconduct report** is a document charging an inmate with a specific rule infraction. If inmates are found guilty, institutional sanctions disqualify them from conjugal visitation and may result in further disciplinary action. By maintaining clear conduct, many medium-security inmates can earn their way into lower-security facilities. The majority of the prisons built since 1950 have been medium-security prisons.

Minimum-security prisons represent the lowest level of institutional security available. Minimum-security prisons provide inmates with great amounts of freedom and autonomy. Minimum-security prison inmates have either been convicted of nonviolent or relatively nonserious offenses or earned a reduced security classification through clear conduct. A stipulation often required for placement in a minimum-security prison is that the inmate be " short." Being **"short "** is a prison term that refers to the time remaining on an inmate's sentence. Generally, an inmate must have fewer than 36 months before parole or discharge to be placed in a minimum-security prison. **Parole** refers to the release of an inmate back into society on a provisional basis. Thus, a paroled inmate will have specific conditions that he or she must abide by to remain in the community. A paroled inmate will also be required to meet frequently with a parole officer. A **parole officer** is a correctional official who supervises parolees within the community and ensures that parolees are abiding by their release agreement. Failure by a parolee to abide by these conditions will result in the revocation of the parole agreement and the inmate may be required to serve the remainder of his/her sentence in prison. **Discharge** is an unconditional release from prison. A discharged inmate has no conditions on his/her release nor does he/she report to any correctional authority. Housing in the minimum-security prison is often dormitory-style, with inmates having a great deal of contact with one another. Because of the dormitory setting, inmates must be able to get along well with others. Fewer security staff work at these prisons, since the inmate population is low-risk.

Inmates in minimum-security prisons are also expected to participate in treatment programs. Reform-driven courses are open to all interested inmates. Similarly, many minimum-security prisons have adopted work and school release programs that permit those who are eligible to leave the institution on furlough. A **furlough** is a temporary release that permits an inmate to work or attend school. This helps normalize the prison environment and eases the inmate's transition back to society. Furloughs not only allow working inmates to contribute to their institutional savings accounts to assist with postrelease expenses, but may also permit inmates to complete a substantial number of credits toward a college degree or certificate. Sometimes, furloughs are granted for a bedside visit to a terminally ill relative or to attend the funeral service of a family member. Furloughs can be **escorted** (requiring the presence of an accompanying prison official) or **unescorted** (not requiring the presence of an accompanying correctional official). Unescorted furloughs place a great deal of trust in the inmate by requiring him/her to return voluntarily to the prison when the furlough expires. It is the minimum-security prison that specifically seeks to assist inmates in their transition from the highly controlled environment found within the maximum- or medium-security prison to an environment that more closely resembles free society. This, in turn, eases their transition into society, making it less problematic (table 2.4).

While the terms "maximum," "medium," and "minimum" have long been used to describe the various security levels of the prison, many jurisdictions are replacing these terms with newer ones. For example, prisons nationwide are now being designated Level 3 (maximum-security), Level 2 (medium-security), or Level 1 (minimum-security) facilities. While this newer approach is gaining popularity, exact labels vary by jurisdiction. For example, California designated Pelican Bay State Prison a Level 4 institution (elevated maximum security), while the Federal Bureau of Prisons (the federal prison system, which operates more than 100 correctional facilities nationwide) classified Marion a Level 6 (supermax) institution. The federal system classifies all its institutions on a scale where Levels 6 and 5 are maximum security, Levels 4 through 2 are medium security, and Level 1 is minimum security. Not only do these labels vary between jurisdictions, but they are also more difficult to understand than the traditional approach. Thus, correctional employees as well as the average citizen tend to prefer the traditional approach since it clearly reveals an institution's security level and helps describe its inmate population. For example, most citizens understand that supermax and maximum-security

TABLE 2.4. Typical Prison Characteristics

Characteristic	Supermax	Maximum	Medium	Minimum
Inmate risk	Extreme	High	Moderate	Low
Rehab programs	None	Limited	Limited	Frequent
Cells	Single	1 or 2 person	1 or 2 person	Dorm
Recreation opportunities	None	Few	Many	Many
Visitation	No contact	Limited	Limited*	Limited*

Source: Jarvis, 1978.

*Conjugal contact permitted by some prisons.

prisons seek to control and incapacitate the offender. Furthermore, they intuitively know what types of prisoners are found within these institutions. However, few can identify the operational objectives of a Level 3 facility or are familiar with the types of prisoners housed therein. While this example pertains to the higher-security institution, similar observations can also be made for medium- and minimum-security prisons.

Although new approaches to classifying prison security levels are confusing to many, conventional wisdom suggests that new prison labeling processes should clearly provide some operational advantage. However, new approaches provide no discernible benefit. In addition to creating confusion, new approaches further distance the prison from its own traditions. This makes it increasingly difficult for the contemporary prison to recognize and appreciate its own history. You may question such a bold statement, as well you should. But think for a moment. One of the core characteristics of the correctional profession has been the way it has classified its prisons. It did so in an open and easily understandable fashion. The new labeling approach accomplishes the same objective as did the old approach but in a less transparent fashion. Such an approach further weakens an already weak link that should clearly exist between the contemporary prison and its historical counterpart. This new approach signifies an attempt to replace many of the older correctional traditions with newer ones. This movement can be most clearly seen when we consider ways to measure prison performance. Should we assess the contemporary prison by the same standard that we used to measure the performance of its predecessor? To answer this question, let us turn our attention to the movement that is underway to replace recidivism as a recognized and accepted performance measure.

Recidivism

Recidivism is no longer the practitioner's preferred method of measuring prison performance

Traditionally, a prison's performance was measured by the recidivism rate of its inmates. The **recidivism rate** refers to the percentage of paroled or discharged inmates who are subsequently convicted of a new crime.

A new conviction may occur anywhere from a few months to 20 or more years after release. Since reconviction can occur anytime, it becomes important to determine the length of time that is to be considered when measuring these rates. For example, some suggest that we measure recidivism in time frames that range from half a year to a year and a half. If an inmate were to remain conviction-free for 6, 12, or 18 months then the prison would be in a good position to take credit for the inmate's success. The problem with short time spans is that they provide little insight into imprisonment's long-term effect on behavior. This is precisely why the time frame for measuring recidivism should ideally be open-ended. By open-ended I am suggesting that there be no specific time frame under consideration. Any reconviction should be considered significant whether it occurs 6 months or 50 years after release—each provides valuable information and aids in assessing institutional performance. Through an open-ended approach,

- we obtain information about the prison's short-term and long-term effect on behavior,
- we are able to identify those periods that may be especially troublesome for the ex-inmate,
- the public's long-term safety is placed at the forefront of the prison's operational objectives, and
- a basis is established for comparative analysis regarding the "performance" of individual prisons.

Recidivism rates have traditionally been accepted as the best measure available to gauge the effects of incarceration on our inmate populations. When considering recidivism, one must recognize that incarceration always has an effect on inmate behavior and subsequently the behavior of the ex-inmate. The prison changes inmates for either the better or the worse. If the effect is negative, it will be reflected in high recidivism rates. But if the effect is positive, it will result in lower recidivism rates. Since recidivism rates are now higher than they have ever previously been, arguments persist for limiting the time frame under consideration. Of course, the shorter the time frame, the more successful the prison appears to the politician and taxpayer. Conversely, longer time frames tend to make the prison appear less effective. It is simple mathematics: the longer the period of time under consideration the greater the opportunity for criminality. Since 90 percent of the inmate population will eventually return to society, reduced recidivism extending over an entire lifetime would contribute more significantly to the public's welfare than if an ex-inmate were to remain conviction-free for just a few short months. An open-ended approach provides knowledge that may serve as the foundation for reducing recidivism rates over long periods.

> *What if . . . the citizenry were to demand that prison performance be measured by recidivism rates? Would the focus of the contemporary prison significantly change? Why?*

As stated, recidivism is no longer the practitioner's preferred method for measuring prison performance. Instead, practitioners and some penologists have used high recidivism rates to condemn reform initiatives and to justify no-frills incarceration. The rationale behind this approach is flawed, since recidivism rates will likely remain high until inmate reform is aggressively sought. The prison is now experiencing what is commonly referred to as a "catch-22." A **catch-22** occurs when a specific objective is desired but is not attainable until some other event that relies on achieving the objective has occurred. For example, the prison desires low recidivism rates, but it is unlikely that recidivism rates will decrease until inmate reform is pursued—but inmate reform will not be pursued until falling recidivism rates establish the value of existing reform initiatives. Confusing, isn't it? Circular dilemmas of this kind are found throughout the prison system. While prison officials are using high recidivism rates to further distance themselves from inmate reform, I use them to condemn prison officials for not providing enough quality programs to equip reform-minded inmates with the tools they need to remain crime-free upon release.

Furthermore, current correctional sentiment maintains that an institution's internal characteristics rather than its performance (i.e., recidivism rates) are legitimate factors for assessing its social value. But what characteristic should be evaluated? How about capacity levels? In fact, this is the characteristic that is currently being advocated. The problem with using capacity levels to assess the prison is that proponents of this approach fail to recognize that community safety is best achieved through long-term intervention strategies. Incapacitating large numbers of offenders without attempting to reform them is a short-term strategy. Yes, it protects society from further predation by a "group" of offenders, but it does this on a temporary basis. Long-term forms of intervention are those approaches that seek to reform the offender so that upon release he/she is less likely to reoffend. Of these two, we are currently pursuing short-term approaches to the exclusion of long-term objectives. We would do well to remember that long-term strategies produce both a short-term effect on crime through incarceration as well as a long-term effect through rehabilitation. Through the pursuit of long-term strategies, both society and the inmate would benefit. Currently, those prisons considered the most successful house the greatest number of offenders. Since we now imprison approximately 7,250 citizens per 100,000, it is understandable that some individuals see capacity levels as a legitimate characteristic for assessment.

While the movement to assess the prison's value by capacity level alone provides a simple and easily quantifiable measure of "performance," it nonetheless lessens our ability to determine imprisonment's long-term impact on public safety. Furthermore, it has a number of additional consequences for both the prison and inmate. Overcrowding produces extremely violent prisons. There is little doubt that prison violence has now reached epidemic proportions. Prison officials are now practicing double bunking. **Double bunking** occurs when two inmates are placed in a cell originally intended to house only one. Some jurisdictions even practice triple bunking, and others place inmates on cots or mattresses in hallways, gymnasiums, and cafeterias, all as a way to increase capacity. Capacity has a number of meanings. First, **rated capacity** refers to the number of beds that a particular prison is permitted to have based upon code or inspection. Next, **operating capacity** refers to the number of inmates a prison can ideally manage based upon its existing staff, kitchen, and medical facilities . Finally, **designed capacity** refers to the total number of inmates a particular prison was intended to house based upon its original blueprint. As presented within this book, the term "capacity" most closely pertains to the latter. So why does a correlation exist between institutional crowding and violence? Before I provide the answer, reconsider for a moment the riots that occurred at

Attica and Santa Fe. One factor cited as a cause for each of these tragic events was severe overcrowding. At the time of Attica's riot, 2,243 inmates were crammed into a facility originally designed to house just 1,200. Santa Fe, while originally designed to house 850 inmates, was at the time of the riot housing 1,158. Overcrowding produces violence because it breeds competition for such scarce resources as job and recreational opportunities, staff attention, and even personal space. Competition of any kind breeds aggression, especially when no alternative course of action exists or when other actions may be considered a sign of weakness. In other words, in an overcrowded prison where competition for limited resources is high, aggression and violence are the only options available to protect one's interests. Failure to act aggressively may itself invite aggression. Generally, lower levels of violence are observable in prisons that are less crowded.

Another reason overcrowding leads to violence is that increases in inmate populations have far outpaced similar increases in numbers of security staff. Each correctional officer is now supervising more inmates than ever before. Yes, cameras have helped address this problem, but they are no substitute for staff. Cameras are unable to interact with inmate populations, resolve conflicts, or instruct inmates on proper forms of interaction. Growing inmate populations reduce the likelihood that officers will detect and intervene in potentially violent situations. Thus, opportunities for inmates to witness the proper use of nonviolent verbal and interpersonal skills as demonstrated by staff are minimized. Violence has become such a regular occurrence in the prison that it seldom commands the attention of those inmates who are in close proximity to an actual attack. In fact, I have witnessed brutal assaults where inmates within just a couple feet of the attack continued with their game of checkers or their conversations—never looking to see what the nearby commotion or pleas for help were about. Attacks happen so often that they no longer have a "shock value." Instead many inmates have become desensitized to aggressive and violent behavior. Once desensitized, a particular inmate is more likely to act inappropriately. Reform also becomes much more difficult to achieve. But what happens to you or me when these "desensitized" inmates are paroled or discharged? Will we become the targets of their aggression and violence? Incarcerating large numbers of offenders and having them supervised by a relatively small number of officers conditions inmates to use aggression and violence as "normal" forms of interaction—the very type of behavior that we want them to avoid.

> *What if . . . institutional violence contributed to the use of violence by ex-inmates? How could we address this issue?*

As might be expected, crowding has other effects as well. Large inmate populations force prison officials to reduce or eliminate most treatment programs. In lieu of education and vocational courses, administrators must divert their time and energy toward maintaining and controlling growing inmate populations. A large inmate population requires a redistribution of financial resources. Since reform initiatives are expensive and are often viewed as "nonessential," they have been targeted for reduction. Contemporary inmates are now experiencing major reductions in treatment programming. Reductions in treatment programming coupled with increased incarceration rates are often referred to as human warehousing. **Human warehousing** refers to the practice of incarcerating large numbers of inmates but giving them little opportunity to engage in productive activities. Instead inmates are filed away and largely forgotten about until their parole or discharge date. With little opportunity for vocational, educational, or counseling pursuits and with large amounts of unoccupied time to contend with, inmates become frustrated. It is this frustration that tends to produce further violence. Overcrowding, competition, and idleness are key ingredients of aggression. It is the violence that results from these conditions that contributes to (for lack of a better term) security inflation. **Security inflation** refers to the tendency of prison officials increasingly to emphasize security measures as a means to maintain control over frustrated inmate populations. The need to maintain control over frustrated inmate populations translates into fewer opportunities for the inmate to engage in productive pursuits. However, it is the lack of productive pursuits that feeds the need for additional control. Talk about your catch-22! Security inflation is especially damaging to the inmate population (and ultimately to society) since it further distances the prison from its reform mandate, making its operational approach one-sided. Without a balanced approach to its operations, the prison truly becomes little more than a human warehouse.

> *What if . . . prison populations were drastically reduced? Would*
> *practitioners begin to reemphasize inmate reform?*

From a citizen's perspective, recidivism is simply the best measure available to assess prison performance as it relates to the promotion of public safety. While recidivism and a concern for public safety are hallmarks of a reform ideology, such an ideology has largely been abandoned by today's correctional official and replaced with a desire simply to "contain and control" the inmate population. The new measure of a prison's performance and a popular way to demonstrate its immediate social value is through its ability to house large numbers of inmates. This newer approach has thrown the prison into a downward spiral of inmate warehousing and security inflation. In essence, this newer approach disavows any concern for the long-term welfare of either the inmate or society. The prison now largely exists only in the present, with little concern for what may occur in the future. Of course, without the tempering effect of reform ideology, prison conditions have also steadily deteriorated.

Over the past 40 years, growing prison populations and deteriorating institutional conditions have prompted inmates to turn to the judiciary for relief. Inmates have traditionally sought judicial assistance by filing lawsuits. These lawsuits have often represented a last-ditch effort to remedy an unfavorable situation. All inmate lawsuits specifically assert that a constitutional right has in some way been violated. Lawsuits require the judiciary to make a determination of fact and when necessary provide a remedy. In the past, inmates were given a great deal of access to the judiciary. Prison reformers and civil rights advocates believed that this access would help ensure ethical and humane treatment. Accountability to the judiciary was seen as the most appropriate way to ensure operational transparency. **Operational transparency** refers to the ability of the judiciary to oversee and, when necessary, direct prison operations. In a broader sense, it also refers to the citizen's ability to "know" what is occurring in tax-supported institutions. Operational transparency from the administrator's viewpoint proves costly in terms of preparing a legal defense. The associated cost of defense preparation is seen by many as an unnecessary drain on scarce correctional resources. Furthermore, there is a growing belief among politicians that a substantial number of inmate lawsuits are baseless. Costs and baseless lawsuits have led to the placement of restrictions on an inmate's access to the judiciary. For example, the **Civil Rights of Institutionalized Person's Act** (CRIPA) largely replaces judicial review with internal (institutional) grievance procedures. Grievance procedures are institutional processes for resolving disputes outside the judicial arena. Proponents of limiting an inmate's access to the judiciary want to internalize grievance processes, replacing legal decisions with what many refer to as **"administrative whims."** This approach reduces operational transparency by forcing inmates to seek a determination of fact from the very people to whom the allegation pertains. This allows prison officials to act in any manner that they themselves deem appropriate, free from external review. This compromises the "checks-and-balances" system upon which our government was founded. A **checks-and-balances** system separates governmental powers into three distinct branches. This ensures that one branch never becomes too powerful. Furthermore, it allows the judiciary to determine the constitutionality of laws and practices. If the judiciary's ability to determine the constitutionality of a particular branch's acts is curtailed, little stands between that branch and its ability to oppress or mistreat the people. This approach is making legal precedent and laws less important to prison operations than administrative decisions. This shift is significant since it establishes a "closed system." A **closed system** refers to an operational process that is undertaken in a secretive or covert fashion. I use the word "secretive" since both the grievance and its findings remain unknown to those outside the prison. This approach reduces the accountability of the prison official and increases the likelihood that inmates will be abused. After all, in the absence of judicial censure, what deterrent exists to ensure the proper treatment of inmate populations?

Similarly, the **Prison Litigation Reform Act** (PLRA), signed into law by former president **Bill Clinton** as part of the **Balanced Budget Downpayment Act II** (HR 3019, Omnibus Appropriations Bill), now requires inmates to pay fees when filing lawsuits. Historically, these fees have been waived as a courtesy. This courtesy was extended to those individuals whom the court determined to be **indigent**. An indigent was anyone who could not easily afford to pay the costs associated with filing a complaint. In addition to the inmate, other indigents included the homeless, the unemployed, and the retired. Fees were waived for these people to ensure that the poor and disenfranchised enjoyed the same constitutional protections as the middle and upper classes. Without waiver, a large percentage of the population could not enjoy the judiciary's protection. PLRA also prohibits inmates who have had previous lawsuits dismissed as frivolous or malicious from further filings. **Frivolous** or **malicious lawsuits** are those that are filed for entertainment or retaliatory purposes. When lawsuits are filed for retaliatory purposes, the inmate is seeking retribution against a prison or its staff for an action or decision perceived as unfair. Both CRIPA and PLRA are significant since they reveal a move by the legislative branch to limit an inmate's ability to seek judicial intervention. It is interesting to note that during the first year under PLRA, the number of inmate lawsuits diminished by nearly 35 percent. Senators **Kennedy** and **Simon** expressed concern about this approach during senatorial debate on March 19, 1996:

> Mr. President, I rise to express my deep concern about the Title VIII of the pending appropriations bill, the so-called Prison Litigation Reform Act (PLRA). . . . PLRA is a far-reaching effort to strip Federal courts of the authority to remedy unconstitutional prison conditions. . . . Finally, I note with great concern that the bill would set a dangerous precedent for stripping the federal courts of the ability to safeguard the civil rights of powerless and disadvantaged groups. (Senator Kennedy)

> Mr. President, I join Senator Kennedy in raising my strong concerns about the Prison Litigation Reform Act. . . . In attempting to curtail frivolous prisoner lawsuits, this litigation goes much too far, and instead may make it impossible for the Federal Courts to remedy constitutional and statutory violations in prisons, jails, and juvenile detention facilities. . . . No doubt there are prisoners who bring baseless suits that deserve to be thrown out of court. But unfortunately, in many instances there are legitimate claims that deserve to be addressed. . . . In seeking to curtail frivolous lawsuits, we cannot deprive individuals of their basic civil rights. We must find the proper balance. (Senator Simon)

In addition to reducing frivolous and malicious lawsuits, CRIPA and PLRA

- insulate the prison from negative publicity in the event that an unconstitutional act has occurred,
- reduce the need for corrections officials to mount rigorous and costly legal defenses, and
- reduce court-ordered judgments.

While a prison's administration may look favorably upon the effects of these two acts, I have heard inmates express a great deal of concern. Inmates generally contend that CRIPA and PLRA

- have effectively limited their ability to obtain a fair and impartial review of grievances,
- have made it more difficult for them to communicate with outside officials,
- have set the stage for increasingly inhumane treatment,
- have reduced the accountability of the executive branch,
- punish all inmates for the actions of a few "irresponsible" ones who occasionally misuse the judiciary, and
- have placed a hardship upon inmates with regard to the paying of filing fees.

While the full effects of CRIPA and PLRA are yet to be seen, there is little doubt that these two acts are making it possible for prisons to operate free of judicial interference. While these acts reduce operating costs and the associated burden of mounting expensive legal defenses, they nonetheless place inmates at a greater risk for civil rights violations. A prison system that operates free of judicial review is a prison system that should be feared.

Observations

As Senators Kennedy and Simon observed, limiting the ability of prisoners to seek judicial protection places the civil rights of our inmate populations at risk. As if this were not bad enough, the public's knowledge about unconstitutional acts occurring within our prisons will subsequently decrease. History has repeatedly shown that any organization that is free to act autonomously will do so with little or no concern about the effects of its actions on the individual. Without the protection of the judiciary, the inmate will be mistreated. Decreasing the ability of the inmate to petition the judiciary creates conditions that are favorable for inmate commodification. **Commodification** refers to viewing inmates as a group and not as unique individuals. When approached in this manner, inmates become little more than objects—objects without needs, feelings, personalities, or even civil rights. By objectifying individuals, the prison and its staff are free to treat these "objects" any way they please. Many of the great tragedies of recent history have occurred when people were objectified: the Jewish Holocaust, the holocausts in Rwanda and Cambodia. Individuals linked to each of these atrocities rationalized their actions by claiming that their victims were "less than human." Each of these events involved unspeakable cruelty and each involved the objectification of entire groups of people who were powerless. The point that I wish to make is that objectification permits both individuals and organizations to act cruelly and without concern for the greater good of society. With regard to the prison, commodification and objectification are part and parcel of a larger warehousing approach where inmates are simply caged for extremely long periods of time with little opportunity to engage in productive pursuits. I have seen the effects of this approach on the inmate. I often tell my students that some inmates end up behaving much like caged tigers. Given enough time, boredom, frustration, and a lack of stimulation produce neurotic inmates who endlessly pace their cells from one end to the other—reminiscent of the tiger that paces its cage. This approach indicates little concern for either the inmate or society. Clearly, the relationship between the inmate and the prison is rapidly changing, as is the relationship between the prison and society. No longer is the prison an institution that seeks to improve the inmate and promote social health; instead, the contemporary prison's primary objective is to house large numbers of inmates as efficiently as possible. Efficiency in turn requires that treatment, counseling, and educational initiatives be reduced or totally eliminated. When institutional decisions are based upon financial considerations alone, objectification and civil rights infringements become common.

While the results of the current approach have yet to be fully experienced, suffice it to say that the outcome will, in all probability, be detrimental to society's long-term interests.

Furthermore, penologists and practitioners must again realize the value of considering recidivism as a performance measure. Recidivism provides a degree of insight into prison operations that is simply unavailable from any other measure. For the lower-security prison, recidivism rates gauge inmate reform, while in the higher-security prison, recidivism rates measure deterrence. Recidivism is the only measure I am aware of that assesses the prison's ability to promote society's long-term interests. If we agree on this point, then perhaps we can also agree that just as the hospital is evaluated on its ability to detect and cure illness and the school is evaluated on its ability to produce students who score highly on standardized exams, prisons should likewise be evaluated on their ability to improve society. What I am proposing is that each prison's performance be measured and assessed against the performance of all other prisons. This is especially useful when the objective of a prison is inmate reform. Assessment of this kind is the impetus for change and improvement, both of which are needed by the prison.

Summary

The prison is a social institution that deals primarily with young males. Since the "typical" inmate is a young male, it is commonly believed that he is both aggressive and violent. However, a substantial proportion of the inmate population is housed at the minimum security level. To be housed at the minimum security level an inmate must have been convicted of a relatively minor offense or have shown little or no propensity toward violence. Low- and medium-security prisons were arguably intended to normalize the prison environment by emphasizing inmate responsibility. These prisons were also intended to provide opportunities for inmate improvement. When comparing lower-security prisons with higher-security prisons, it becomes apparent that there is a dichotomy in the underlying operational objectives of our penal institutions. In the supermax and maximum-security prisons, rehabilitation has been deserted. Instead these institutions emphasize the containment and control of the offender. In the minimum- and medium-security institutions, rehabilitation is both underemphasized and at grave risk for complete abandonment—but it is still there, existing largely in a dormant state. Regardless of the security level being considered, recidivism as a measure of the prison's ability to promote public safety has largely been replaced by a consideration of the prison's ability to house increasing inmate populations. While this approach may promote the public's short-term welfare by incapacitating increasing percentages of the offender population, it may actually contribute to crime rates by exposing many nonserious offenders to those who are more hardened. The influence that these serious offenders exert over the less experienced offender should not be underestimated. Often this influence is powerful and quite negative. Furthermore, these less serious offenders are exposed to overcrowded prison conditions that require them to compete directly with the hardened offender for scarce resources. Competition leads to intimidation, aggression, and even violence. Once exposed to this type of environment, inmates (especially those who are nonserious) become embittered and desensitized to brutality—which does not benefit society. Perhaps the key to effectively promoting public safety can be found in **prison specialization**. Prison specialization refers to assigning each prison a particular objective. For example, one prison might be delegated the task of strict incapacitation while another pursues inmate reform. Prison specialization is the topic of the next chapter.

Chapter Highlights

1. Historically, the offender was viewed as both the physical and mental equivalent of a caveman.
2. It was initially surmised that if the body appeared primitive so too was the intellect.
3. Offenders and nonoffenders are often more similar than dissimilar.
4. Many inmates are incarcerated in minimum-security prisons— suggesting that they have been convicted of relatively minor offenses and have shown little propensity toward violence.
5. Supermax prisons represent the highest level of institutional security ever developed.

6. The primary objective of the maximum-security prison, much like the supermax, is to control and incapacitate inmates.

7. Most medium-security prisons provide limited opportunities for education, employment, and recreational activities.

8. Conjugal visits provide an incentive for married inmates to maintain clear conduct.

9. Minimum-security prisons represent the lowest level of institutional security available.

10. Furloughs provide inmates an opportunity to work and save for post-release expenses.

11. Traditionally, an institution's effectiveness was measured in recidivism rates.

12. A correlation exists between institutional crowding and violence.

13. Contemporary incarceration has become little more than human warehousing where few opportunities exist for self-improvement.

14. A closed prison system increases the likelihood for inmate abuse.

15. Recent legislative acts have significantly curtailed the judiciary's ability to oversee prison operations.

16. Prison administrators prefer internal to external forms of conflict resolution—this minimizes negative publicity and reduces the cost associated with preparing a legal defense.

17. Recidivism is a performance measure that allows a prison to be rank-ordered in relation to its peer institutions.

Discussion Questions

1. Why would early criminologists link physical traits to behavior? Is there a correlation?

2. What are the characteristics of the typical inmate? Do these characteristics suggest a propensity toward violence?

3. How do supermax and maximum-security prisons differ from medium- and minimum-security prisons? Does each have the same overall objective of community safety and, if so, why do they approach this objective differently?

4. Does each of the institutions referenced in question 3 have a proper place within our prison system? Why or why not?

5. Which security level is more conducive to punishment and deterrence? Why?

6. Which security level is more conducive to rehabilitation? Why?

7. What is the relationship between prison crowding and violence?

8. Does inmate warehousing hinder the prison's ability to effectively promote long-term public safety?
9. Does a closed prison system increase the likelihood for inmate abuse? Why or why not?
10. What are the benefits, if any, of using recidivism as a measure of prison performance?
11. In your opinion should each prison be assessed on its recidivism rate? Why or why not?
12. Would recidivism rates prove to be an effective measure of inmate reform? How about specific deterrence? Explain.

Sources

Bureau of Justice Statistics. 2003. *Census of State and Federal Correctional Facilities, 2000.* Washington, DC: U.S. Department of Justice.

Criminal Justice Institute. 2000. *The 1998 Corrections Yearbook: Adult Corrections.* Middleton, CT.

Harrison, Paige M., and Allen J. Beck. 2005. *Prison and Jail Inmates at Midyear 2004.* Washington, DC: U.S. Department of Justice.

Jarvis, Dwight. 1978. *Institutional Treatment of the Offender.* New York: McGraw-Hill Publishing.

Montgomery, R., Jr., and G. Crews. 1998. *A History of Correctional Violence: An Examination of Reported Causes of Riots and Disturbances.* Lanham, MD: American Correctional Association.

Riveland, Chase, 1999. *Supermax Prisons: Overview and General Considerations.* Washington, DC: U.S. Department of Justice.

Stephan, J. J., and J. C. Karberg. 2003. *Census of State and Federal Correctional Facilities, 2002.* Washington, DC: U.S. Department of Justice.

Most inmates appreciate opportunities for treatment.

Chapter Three

Classification and Prison Specialization

The observation appearing on the preceding page contains a profound logic that serves as the basis for this chapter. To understand the importance of this statement one must recognize that the word "most" suggests that there are two distinct groups of inmates. These two groups comprise those inmates who are favorably disposed to treatment and those that are not. Those who are favorably disposed to treatment are considered to be amenable. **Amenability** refers to an inmate's desire to undergo treatment as a reformative measure. Reform, or one's ability to change for the better, requires that an inmate grasps the error of his/her ways, identifies patterns of problematic behavior, and pursues an appropriate course of action to resolve criminogenic issues. Often, counseling as well as education and vocational endeavors will provide the knowledge and skills necessary for reform—but it is the acknowledgment of wrongdoing that is often the most significant step in this process.

Amenability is a necessary consideration when determining whether an inmate is "changeable" or "unchangeable." If an inmate is amenable, he/she is likely to benefit from treatment. I will refer to these inmates as "changeables." If an inmate is not amenable, he/she will not benefit from treatment. I will refer to these inmates as "unchangeables." Since change can occur only with the inmate's cooperation and participation, reform initiatives must specifically target changeable inmates. Inmates are generally quite clear about where they stand on the topic of rehabilitation. They either acknowledge a need for treatment or refuse to recognize its value. Those in the latter group often formulate a series of excuses for their conduct and disavow any need for reform. Still others suffer from mental or emotional conditions that render them, perhaps temporarily, incapable of participation. To force treatment upon the unchangeable inmate is inappropriate, costly, and of no benefit to society.

Since there are two categories of inmate, the changeable and the unchangeable, it stands to reason that it might be counterproductive to house both within the same prison. Why? The answer is simple. Housing these two groups of inmates within the same prison provides the unchangeable inmate an opportunity to disrupt the treatment processes of those who desire reform. Often, unchangeable inmates want to control those who are young, impressionable, and easily manipulated—in other words, the changeable inmate. Unchangeables often discourage participation in treatment programs through intimidation. When this occurs, the prison becomes little more than a breeding ground for criminality. In other words, those inmates who might be reformed are lost to the control of the hardened offender. They may in turn become unchangeable themselves. To improve the effectiveness of the prison, each inmate must be classified as either changeable or unchangeable and placed in an appropriate facility. This, as you might expect, requires that each prison be equipped to deal with one but not both groups. Thus, the concept of prison specialization emerges. I am not the first to suggest "specialized prisons." Yet, as a contemporary method for promoting public safety, this proposal has largely been ignored. I have yet to see another present-day scholar use the phrase "prison specialization" or publicly address this subject. Nonetheless, the underlying concept has existed for many years. Since no contemporary penologist that I am familiar with has written about this subject, I often find myself rummaging through older texts and monographs to locate related materials. It was during one of these rummaging forays that I found a text entitled *Correctional Institutions* (1970). This text embodies the writings of noted penologists such as **Thorsten Sellin, Richard McGee, John Irwin, Daniel Glaser, Donald Cressey,** and **Gilbert Geis**. They have directly or indirectly helped shape my views on this subject. But, more important, I discovered a chapter by **Howard Gill** entitled "Correctional Philosophy and Architecture." This chapter's title is somewhat misleading since inmate classification and the establishment of specialty prisons is its subject. Although it has now been over 30 since its publication, Gill's chapter remains the most significant work on prison specialization to date. Gill's writings help form the foundation for the remainder of this chapter.

> *What if . . . changeable and unchangeable inmates were housed separately? Would recidivism rates improve?*

The Contemporary Approach

Before proceeding, it is necessary briefly to review modern classification practices to determine how they mesh with the prison's traditional objectives. These traditional objectives provide a degree of insight into how the prison was originally designed to operate. The problem, however, is that many practitioners find it difficult to identify the historical goals of the prison. This creates a disjunct between the prison's history and present-day practices. For many practitioners, the only objective that is readily identifiable is containment. This is unfortunate since it indicates a lack of familiarity of the practitioners with the history upon which their profession was established. Without a clear understanding of whence a profession has come, it is difficult for its members to control its evolution intelligently. It is this lack of familiarity with the traditional objectives of the prison that is partially responsible for the prison's abandonment of a reform ideology. This is particularly noticeable in modern **inmate classification** processes. Originally, inmate classification involved a team of correctional professionals, including psychologists, educators, administrators, and security personnel. These individuals were tasked with determining an inmate's treatment and security requirements. Shortly after arriving at a prison, each inmate was required to meet with the classification committee. At this initial meeting, prison officials could assess the inmate's needs and determine how his/her presence might affect the institution. An inmate's past criminal record was considered, as were gang affiliations, educational attainment, family and employment histories, and demeanor. This process allowed prison personnel to design an appropriate course of action to address an inmate's needs. Thus, if an inmate had an anger management problem, a counseling program would be developed to help rectify anger issues. Furthermore, if an inmate lacked the skills necessary to obtain and maintain employment, then a course of action would be prescribed to develop appropriate skills. Of course, this approach was reform oriented and emulated the **medical process** by which a diagnosis must precede treatment and a cure. In this sense, the classification committee was akin to a board of physicians diagnosing a condition or sickness. The goal of this committee was to increase public safety through the identification and treatment of individual-level needs. In addition to determining an appropriate course of treatment, classification processes were also used to determine an inmate's security requirements. This portion of the process was used to decide housing and work assignments and to alert appropriate staff to any security-related matters. The overall objective of this portion of the process was to promote inmate and staff safety. Thus, classification has historically functioned with a concern for both inmate treatment and institutional security. These dual concerns served to balance the interests of the inmate and society with interests that were primarily institutionally oriented. While current classification approaches are quite similar, they have largely abandoned reform initiatives, making classification little more than a mechanism that is used to determine an inmate's security rating. Such an approach runs counter to traditional penal ideology and practice. Consider the following statement addressing the responsibility of the prison to provide treatment:

> The public welfare can best be protected by returning as many prisoners as possible to the community fitted educationally and vocationally, in physical and mental health and through changed attitudes and ideals, to take their places as law-abiding citizens. The necessity for an institutional program, which will have a constructive effect upon prisoners, is based upon the inescapable fact that over ninety-five percent of all prisoners committed to prison are sooner or

later returned to the community. The prison has the grave responsibility of determining whether they shall be returned less criminally inclined or with criminal attitudes more fixed and with criminal abilities more fully developed. (*Handbook on Classification*, p. 1)

This statement clearly reveals the importance that penologists have traditionally placed on inmate reform both as an operational objective and as a goal of the classification process. Early scholars often warned prison administrators not to forget the traditional objectives of the prison—one of which is inmate reform. In the absence of a reform ideology prisons are free to operate with little or no concern for either the inmate or society. Classification processes that are steeped in a reform ideology are operationally, philosophically, and professionally sound. To better understand inmate classification as well as prison specialization let us turn our attention to the Pennsylvania and Auburn systems of prison management. A review of these approaches will serve as a good introduction to Gill's ideas.

Prison Typologies

Many of you may already be familiar with the Pennsylvania and Auburn prison systems. These two approaches to prison management developed in the United States during the antebellum period. Together, these styles of management encapsulate the debate that existed then, as it still does, concerning the prison's objectives. On one side of this debate were those subscribing to reform ideology (Pennsylvania). Proponents of this approach believed that offenders were misguided. Therefore, religious instruction was needed to provide direction and to produce personal reform. Since this approach valued inmate reform, it was interested in the long-term interests of both the inmate and society. On the other side of this debate were those who believed that the prison's primary objective should be efficient and profitable operations (Auburn). This approach, it was reasoned, would help reduce the financial burden placed upon the taxpaying public to maintain its prisons. This approach was interested in meeting the needs of the prison. These approaches also loosely embody the ideologies of normalization and less eligibility.

Let us begin our review with the **Pennsylvania system,** also known as the **"separate system."** Under this style of prison management inmates were isolated from one another and were required to maintain absolute silence. Inmates could easily serve long sentences and never see a fellow inmate or hear another inmate's voice. Upon arrival, inmates were "hooded" to prevent them from communicating or seeing anyone else within the prison. This hood remained on an inmate's head until he entered his cell. Once an inmate entered his individual cell, he remained there until release. Visitation with loved ones was not permitted, nor was communication with the outside world. The only person an inmate was permitted to see was the prison's minister. Advocates of this approach believed that isolation and religious indoctrination would lead to repentance. Of course, an admission of wrongdoing was seen as the first step toward offender reform.

As you may have guessed, the results of this approach were quite the opposite of what was anticipated. Scores of inmates were driven insane. Furthermore, the socialization and communication skills of the inmate population deteriorated noticeably. From a human perspective, this approach proved both cruel and ineffective at promoting reform. In fact, this approach did nothing to prepare inmates for release. Furthermore, those inmates who were eventually released back to society were understandably frustrated and angry. From an institutional perspective, this approach proved financially prohibitive since inmates could do little to offset the prison's operating expenses. In a setting that valued isolation, the only goods that inmates could realistically produce for sale were small wood- or leather-craft items. Two of the most famous institutions that operated under this approach were the **Walnut Street Jail** (1790) and **Eastern Penitentiary** in Pennsylvania (1829). This approach lost favor by 1866 and was replaced by the Auburn system. Despite the failure of this approach, it recognized that reform must start with an inmate's personal desire for change. Without such a desire, reform could not occur.

Unlike the Pennsylvania approach, the **Auburn system** (named after **Auburn Prison** in New York) permitted inmates to congregate and interact while working. Therefore, this approach is often referred to as the **"congregate system."** Even though inmates worked collectively, a strict code of silence was enforced through corporal punishments such as whippings. Work assignments were industrial in nature and involved the production of engines, machinery, boilers, and furniture. The sale of these highly sought-after items often produced healthy profit margins. Efficiency and profit were stressed as correctional objectives. In many ways, the Auburn prison operated much like a factory—the major difference being the captive workforce. Inmates were often required to work six days a week for ten or more hours each day. This approach sent a clear message to the inmate population that their value was not in their humanity but in their ability to provide cheap labor. Such a dehumanizing approach to prison operations was no less problematic than the Pennsylvania approach. While hard labor has traditionally been linked to offender reform, it appears that reform in this instance was secondary to institutional profit. This approach highlights the prison's slow but relentless march toward a style of management that considers the needs of the institution first, with all other considerations being secondary.

The use of the **lockstep** was also popularized under the Auburn style of management. Designed by Deputy Warden **John Cray** (Auburn Prison), the lockstep was used when moving inmates about the prison or its grounds. The lockstep required inmates to form a line, with each inmate being situated directly behind another. On command, each inmate then placed his hands on the shoulders of the inmate in front. When given the order, all inmates began to march in unison. The lockstep allowed officers to maintain control over large numbers of inmates, eliminating the possibility for horseplay and insubordination. The use of the lockstep helped ensure that inmates could be moved efficiently and with few supervising officers. The lockstep has come to symbolize the mobilization of the inmate population for institutional gain. Two of the more noteworthy prisons that used this approach were **Kingston Penitentiary** in Ontario, Canada, and **Sing Sing Prison** in New York. In 1894, New York lawmakers prohibited this type of work arrangement and effectively ended the Auburn style of prison management.

It should be obvious from these divergent styles of management that debate has long existed over how the prison should interact with inmate populations. Questions persist about whether the prison should adhere to a reform ideology or whether it should be more punitively oriented. Furthermore, what happens when one of these objectives is sought to the exclusion of the other? Similarly, should the prison recognize the individuality of each inmate or should it instead approach inmates in the aggregate, mobilizing them for financial gain? Regardless of your answers to these difficult questions, both the Pennsylvania and Auburn styles of management failed to win widespread support because of the intemperate position each assumed. While neither approach is ideal, the congregate system with its emphasis on inmate control and operational efficiency meshes well with current conservative ideology. Table 3.1 helps clarify the differences between these two approaches.

In addition to the Pennsylvania and Auburn styles of prison management, other typologies have been proposed to help categorize prison operations. Let us consider Gill's prison genera. According to Gill, all prisons fit into the following three categories:

- Officials of the **custodial prison** emphasize strict control over inmate populations. Treatment and educational programming are withheld since inmate reform is not an institutional pursuit. Rather, the development of a strong and capable security contingent is highly valued. Uniformed personnel, visible weaponry, high walls, and observation towers are associated with this type of prison.
- **Progressive prisons** create and promote a public perception that reasonable efforts are being made to provide treatment to the inmate population. This "illusion" is created to ward off criticisms of a cold and uncaring prison system. While officials of the progressive prison portray it as a humanitarian institution, in

TABLE 3.1. Pennsylvania and Auburn Prison Systems

	Pennsylvania (separate system)	Auburn (congregate system)
Cell	Single-occupancy	Single-occupancy
Interaction	Complete isolation	Congregation allowed
Emphasis	Inmate reform	Efficiency/profit
Advantages	Concern for society	Profitable operations
Disadvantages	Inmate insanity; expensive	Large numbers of staff; forced labor

reality little effort at reform is made. Even though the progressive prison appears less harsh than the custodial prison, in reality its emphasis is also on inmate containment and control.

- **Professionally oriented prisons** emphasize normalization and inmate responsibility. This type of prison provides properly funded treatment programs that are designed to address each offender's unique needs. While all prisons by their nature must emphasize inmate control, professional prisons temper this approach with a genuine interest in inmate reform.

Let us now consider each of these typologies in greater detail, beginning with the **custodial prison.** As its name implies, the custodial prison is an institution where security and orderly operations are pursued to the exclusion of all other objectives. Staff generally do not consider inmates unique individuals but rather members of a larger group— "the inmate population." The mere status of being an "inmate" entails a loss of identity. This is frequently reflected in the extensive use of institutional numbers. An **institutional number** is a unique string of digits, usually eight to ten characters in length, that is assigned to each inmate for identification purposes. Often, an inmate's institutional number becomes his/her primary identity. Whenever inmates are referred to by a prison official or asked their identity, they are required to provide this number. In effect, this number replaces each inmate's name, ensuring that inmates have no identity apart from that provided by the institution.

Since security is the primary objective of the custodial prison, an emphasis is placed upon the use of structural barriers, including concertina wire, walls, bars, and steel doors, that are designed to control inmate movement and decrease the likelihood of escape. Few opportunities exist for congregate activities (reminiscent of the separate system), with all actions being evaluated for the risk that they pose to the institution. Educational, vocational, and recreational programming that requires inmate movement and assembly is seen as a threat to the security of the prison. These types of activities are limited or prohibited— after all, any time inmates are permitted to move about or to congregate en masse, the opportunity for conflict and insurrection grow. Penologists are increasingly referring to custodial prisons as "human warehouses."

This phrase reflects the approach taken by the custodial prison of simply "storing" inmates until their release dates. Inmates often refer to this style of incarceration as "doing hard time." **Hard time** refers to confinement where few amenities or activities are provided. Without amenities or activities to divert inmate attention away from the harshness of the prison's environment, time is often perceived as being static. Such an approach makes incarceration especially arduous.

Next, is the **progressive prison.** The progressive prison offers educational, vocational, and recreational programming. Even though programming is offered, the emphasis is not on inmate reform but rather on producing and perpetuating an appearance of humanitarianism. This illusion is created to ward off criticism that the prison is a cold and uncaring institution. To most outsiders, prison officials are seen as providing an atmosphere conducive to reform—but in reality officials of these prisons see little intrinsic value in such pursuits. In addition to promoting a positive institutional image these programs serve as management tools. How? The answer is quite simple. Treatment programs tend to occupy a good deal of the inmate population's time. Therefore, they serve as a focal point for their energy. It is believed that idle hands (and minds) are a threat to the institution. Through control of the inmate population's time and energy, inmates have little opportunity to become engaged in pursuits that might otherwise be disruptive to the orderly operation of the institution. Those treatment programs that are being offered, while underfunded and understaffed, primarily serve the needs of the institution rather than the needs or interests of the inmate and society. Nonetheless, the progressive prison has to some degree helped keep the "idea" of inmate reform alive.

The final prison type that Gill recognizes is the **professional prison.** In the professional prison a genuine attempt is made to normalize (to the extent possible) the penal environment. Under normalization an inmate is given considerable freedom and is encouraged to make responsible decisions during his/her term of incarceration. It is believed that if inmates are taught how to make good decisions while imprisoned they will do the same after release. To assist in this process inmates are given opportunities to develop their decision-making skills. To this end, inmates are encouraged to help establish the rules (not security-related ones of course) for their particular housing area. For example, inmates living in a housing unit might be permitted to establish rules pertaining to cleaning duties or recreational schedules for their unit. This opportunity may also, to a limited degree, pertain to the types of disciplinary actions implemented for minor infractions of housing unit rules. Inmate governance is generally welcomed and taken quite seriously. For many inmates this may represent the first opportunity they have had to help shape the actions of an institution. Furthermore, prison administrators regularly solicit suggestions from the inmate population about ways to improve the delivery of services. These services may include those related to food, laundry, visitation, recreation, and treatment. This approach helps soften the harsh prison environment and allows inmates to retain a degree of control over their daily lives. Inmates appreciate having a "say" in how the prison functions, making them more willing to participate in therapeutic programs.

In addition to normalizing the penal environment, professional prisons also provide a wide range of treatment options. Programs are well funded and adequately staffed. Treatment personnel have backgrounds in therapy, counseling and education and hold appropriate certificates and degrees in the areas in which they specialize. These specialty areas include anger management and conflict resolution, interpersonal relationships and sexuality, communication processes, self-image, drug and alcohol addictions, and a host of vocational topics. Proponents of this approach recognize that while treatment and education are expensive, they reduce recidivism and, thereby, justify increased expenditures. Perhaps you have seen the bumper sticker that refers to the high cost of education but then counters by observing that ignorance is even more costly. Proponents of the professional prison claim the same for treatment. Yes, it is expensive, but failing to provide treatment to our offenders proves even more costly.

Treatment programs also help ensure that inmates are prepared to reenter society. Reentry is often the source of a great deal of anxiety, especially when inmates are ill prepared to make such a transition. Therefore, the professional prison pays a great deal of attention to this event. In fact, professional prisons attempt to equip each inmate with the skills necessary for successful social assimilation. Having been the releasing official for many inmates over the years, I have become quite familiar with the anxiety that always accompanies an impending release. As a release date approaches, an inmate tends to become increasingly apprehensive about whether he/she will be welcomed back by family and friends. Just as all inmates experience a "shock" upon entering the prison, all inmates also experience a "shock" when reentering society. Given this, efforts are made to adequately prepare inmates for this event. Part of this preparation entails the realization that inmates frequently become **institutionalized**. When this occurs, an inmate internalizes the role of "being a prisoner," carrying this identity over into his/her postrelease life. Inmates who have become institutionalized may consider themselves "prisoners" years after parole or discharge. Furthermore, they often become overly dependent on those around them. Their worldview may change and they may begin to see threats and hostilities where none exist. Similarly, their ability to cope with life's challenges and stresses may become compromised, making social reentry problematic. Of course, the longer an individual is incarcerated, the greater the effects of institutionalization. Often the effects of institutionalization can be greatly reduced through a prerelease program that addresses this very topic. Now that we have reviewed Gill's prison typologies, let us consider inmate classification in greater detail.

Classification

Classification refers to an evaluative process traditionally involving treatment and security considerations. During this process an inmate's educational level was considered, as was his/her suitability for vocational training. It was also determined whether therapy was appropriate. The overall objective of the treatment portion of this process was the formulation of a plan designed to reform the inmate and benefit society through lower recidivism rates. In addition to a consideration of an inmate's treatment needs, classification has long involved an assessment of the "risks" associated with each inmate. **Risks** are of two kinds: those that pertain to escape and those that threaten the orderly operations of the institution. To identify and minimize risks, prison officials rely upon a risk assessment. A **risk assessment** considers factors such as gang affiliation, past criminal record, and the inmate's propensity toward violence. During this assessment, inmates are also given the opportunity to compile an enemy list. An **enemy list** is a document that identifies all incarcerated enemies of a particular inmate. This list helps to protect inmates from one another, promoting a safer and more secure institution. Depending on the results of this assessment, conditions are often imposed upon the inmate with regard to housing arrangements or the types of activities in which he/she is permitted to participate. For example, if it appears that an inmate is especially violent, he/she might be placed upon restriction. **Restriction** often involves confining an inmate to his/her cell or housing unit. This increases security's ability to supervise particularly obstinate inmates.

Given that classification has traditionally pursued multiple objectives, it should come as no surprise that confusion exists about which objective is most important. Since security must be achieved prior to all other objectives, practitioners tend to forget that reform ideology has historically played a prominent role in the classification process. Uncertainty about the duality of classification's objectives can be found in the ranks of any **initial classification committee** (ICC) or **reclassification committee** (RCC). The ICC is tasked with conducting all preliminary assessments, while the RCC meets whenever an inmate is involved in misconduct or when mandated to do so by policy. Even though both of these committees are composed of treatment and security personnel, they have become neglectful of their reform mandate. Security considerations now dominate classification to the exclusion of treatment. Yes, there are still treatment-oriented personnel who sit on institutional committees, but their presence is largely ceremonial rather than functional. Factors responsible for the current de-emphasis of inmate treatment include overcrowded institutions that necessitate heightened security and a reduction in the number of inmate advocacy groups championing reform.

> *What if . . . prison officials were to value treatment and security objectives equally? Who would benefit from this approach?*

While some practitioners claim that an interest in treatment is antiquated, others realize that treatment and security pursuits are complementary. For example, institutional security is served when treatment programs teach responsible behavior. Similarly, institutional security promotes reform by stressing responsibility and accountability, the cornerstones of reform ideology. Both approaches together promote community safety (albeit differently) and neither objective can be fully achieved without the other. One personal characteristic that can dramatically impact both reform and security pursuits is inmate demeanor. Let us now consider demeanor as a factor that should be taken into account during classification processes.

Inmate Typologies

To better understand classification and its relationship to prison specialization we must acknowledge the importance of inmate demeanor within the treatment process. **Demeanor** refers to an inmate's attitude toward confinement, treatment, and the opportunities that incarceration provides for personal reform. When considering an inmate's demeanor it is necessary for classification specialists to

- determine whether an inmate is interested in reform, and
- determine whether amenable inmates are actually capable (physically, mentally, and emotionally) of such a pursuit.

To promote public safety sufficiently, prison officials must consider an inmate's desire for personal reform as well as his/her ability to complete a treatment program. An assessment of these factors is essential when determining an inmate's classification status. According to Gill, classification labels should reflect each inmate's amenability to treatment. These labels include

- **new**—which denotes inmates who are yet to be interviewed, observed, and classified for proper placement,
- **intractable**—which denotes those inmates who are not interested in or refuse to participate in treatment,
- **tractable**—which denotes those inmates who are definitely interested in treatment, and
- **defective**—which denotes those inmates who are unable to participate in treatment due to a condition that renders participation impossible (conditions may be beyond the inmate's control).

These labels reflect a great deal of diversity in the inmate population's desire and ability to change. If we acknowledge that diversity exists within our inmate population, then we should also concede that generalized institutional placement may be counterproductive to public safety. **Generalized institutional placement** refers to housing inmates of varying demeanors within the same prison. Such a practice allows inmates from each of Gill's categories (intractable, tractable, and defective) to intermingle freely. Permitting intractable and tractable inmates to interact openly represents one of the most flawed penal practices ever adopted, especially since it is based upon the assumption that all inmates are beyond reformation. Furthermore, it permits the intractable inmate to have a corrupting effect upon those inmates who are reformable. To improve the ability of the prison to promote public safety, we must realize that generalized placement allows hardened inmates to actively influence those inmates who are less criminally inclined. Practitioners know firsthand that it is within our prisons that criminal ideas are developed and illicit skills honed. It is common to encounter inmates who boast of their exploits and openly share their criminal techniques with other inmates. It is through the exchange of these ideas, experiences, and techniques that the prison has been transformed into the best "school of crime" available.

To counter the effects of generalized placement, Gill suggests that we separate inmates by demeanor (intractable, tractable, and defective) as well as by risk (maximum, medium, and minimum). Such an approach is absolutely essential if we are to maximize the prison's ability to promote the public's welfare. For example, consider the following observation:

> [T]heory and experience demand the separation of offenders into more or less homogeneous groups. All kinds of individuals are received in prison; experienced, hardened criminals and those who have committed their first offense; the serious escape risk and the person who would leave the institution only by legal process; the adolescent and the aged; the diseased and healthy; the intelligent and the feeble-minded; homosexuals, the insane and psychopathic, and persons who are dangerous to themselves and others. The difficulty in providing a program that will adequately meet the needs and requirements of all these types in one institution is obvious. . . . Efficient segregation is necessary for good custody, discipline and rehabilitation. (*Handbook on Classification*, p. 5)

Having briefly reviewed the classification labels proposed by Gill, let us now consider how each label relates to prison operations. We begin by considering the newly imprisoned offender. This inmate would be designated as **"new"** and initially assigned to a maximum-security prison. Maximum-security placement is necessary while officials determine an inmate's level of risk. Maximum-security prisons would serve as **reception and diagnostic centers** (RDCs). Under Gill's proposal, a reception and diagnostic center is where specialists would determine each inmate's amenability to treatment and his/her security requirement. Using reception and diagnostic staff to make both determinations differs from current approaches where RDC staff largely limit their concerns to security requirements and institutional placements. Thus, the current objective of reception and diagnostic staff is to determine an inmate's security level and whether he/she should be placed into a maximum-, medium-, or minimum-security prison. Of course, inmates who are determined to be "high risk" are placed into maximum-security institutions. Similarly, inmates presenting fewer risks are appropriately housed in medium- or minimum-security prisons. While this practice is standard operating procedure in systems nationwide, it ignores inmate amenability. The amenability of the inmate to treatment is universally disregarded by contemporary practitioners during all stages of incarceration. This disregard for reform is especially evident at the initial stage of incarceration. As a result of ignoring an inmate's amenability to treatment at the reception and diagnostic stage

- little insight (apart from what is needed for security purposes) is obtained into the inmate's cognitive or emotional development or his/her demeanor,
- the inmate's first contact with the prison system is sterile and unconcerned, and
- rehabilitation and treatment are portrayed as having little intrinsic value.

You will notice that several of these observations deal directly with perceptions. Perceptions may affect an inmate's amenability and willingness to pursue or forgo treatment. A lack of concern by RDC staff for inmate reform becomes evident early in the diagnostic process. This lack of interest in treatment is later reinforced by the number, types, and overall quality of the programs being offered in other institutions. To inspire and motivate the inmate, officials must genuinely desire reform and express that concern early in the inmate's term of incarceration. If officials do not subscribe to a reform ideology, inmates will have little incentive to seek personal reform. A prison's lack of interest in treatment often impacts inmates most strongly at the early stages of processing. This is precisely why reception and diagnostic specialists should conduct both treatment and security assessments. In this way, a positive message is sent to the inmate population about their worth as human beings. This approach is desirable when dealing with citizens of a democratic society where it is reasonable for each citizen to expect the government to act in his/her best interest. This expectation includes giving felons an opportunity for self-betterment. This approach is an essential component of prison specialization and would undeniably improve community safety. The label "new" would be temporary, lasting only the duration of the reception and diagnostic process. At that point, an inmate would be given one of the three remaining labels and placed into a prison specifically designed to address his/her needs and security requirements.

The next type of inmate Gill identifies is the **intractable** one. An intractable inmate is obstinate and unruly. From a correctional perspective intractability denotes a refusal to follow an institution's rules. Furthermore, the intractable inmate refuses to acknowledge a need for reform or the value of treatment. Intractability can be determined by considering inmate declarations and through direct observation. A consideration of an inmate's criminal record as well as insight provided by family, friends, and past employers might also prove beneficial in determining which inmates are intractable and which are not. My own experience suggests that intractable inmates refuse to follow rules and acknowledge a personal need for treatment because they

- fail to see their actions as illegal,
- have formulated a number of excuses to justify their actions and minimize their responsibility,
- perceive themselves as victims of the system,
- express allegiance to higher authorities (perhaps a gang),

- are often unable to confide in others, limiting the effectiveness of counseling as a treatment option, or
- may openly question the value of education, training, and treatment.

Since intractables refuse to acknowledge wrongdoing or to participate in institutional programming, they present a danger to the orderly operation of the prison. Much of this danger originates in the large amount of time intractables can devote to disruptive activities. It is for this same reason that intractables also threaten the safety of inmates and staff alike. They have often been described as "predatory inmates," since they actively seek to exploit those around them. According to Gill, incarceration for intractable inmates should be little more than "simple, secure living quarters." In other words, intractables should be provided a humane standard of living, but beyond that little else should be furnished. To do so would be a waste of scarce resources. Since intractables refuse all attempts at reform (either overtly or covertly), may frequently question the legitimacy of the criminal justice system, and tend to challenge authority or incite other inmates to do the same, they are especially dangerous to confine. Therefore, containment and strict physical control are warranted. The most appropriate place to provide the level of control needed for the intractable inmate is the maximum-security prison. Since "new" inmates would also be held in maximum-security facilities, both intractable and new inmates could be housed in separate areas of the same prisons. Maximum-security prisons would then serve two functions: first, as institutions that are designed to house our most dangerous and predatory offenders (intractables) and, second, as reception and diagnostic centers where treatment and security assessments are conducted. As a result of housing intractable inmates in facilities where the bulk of the classification process occurs, intractables would have access to appropriate staff in the event a change in their classification status were to become necessary— especially if an intractable were to expresses a desire for treatment. If this were to occur, reclassification might be required. Reclassification, if determined to be appropriate, would necessitate the development of a treatment plan as well as a change in both an intractable's security designation and institutional placement. It is important to understand that prison specialization seeks to prevent the intractable from coming into contact with other types of inmates. This is due to the intractable's predatory nature and ability to corrupt others. This corrupting influence is especially damaging when it involves tractable inmates.

Unlike the intractable inmate, **tractable** inmates acknowledge a need for treatment. The term "tractable" denotes a personality that is receptive to correction and reform. My experience suggests that a fairly large portion of the inmate population may be tractable. Having worked closely with tractable offenders in a variety of institutional and community settings, I have noticed a consensus about the types of programs they find most beneficial. In general, tractable offenders want treatment that provides

- education and vocational training (to improve opportunities for postrelease employment),
- substance abuse and anger management counseling (since problems in these areas diminish one's ability to maintain employment and sustain positive relationships), and
- life-skills training to include financial management and parenting strategies (since financial and familial stresses are often associated with abuse and substance use).

Since tractable inmates acknowledge a need for treatment they make better candidates for reform than do intractables. Individuals who have worked with inmates know firsthand that reform cannot be forced or finessed. Simply put, if an inmate refuses treatment, it is highly unlikely that a reformed state will be achieved. But how would an inmate's tractability be determined? Well, tractability is determinable in the same manner as intractability—primarily through a consideration of an inmate's statements about reform and through direct observation and insight obtained from family, friends, and former employers. Gill believes that tractable inmates deserve society's full support as evidenced by comprehensive treatment programs. However, institutional treatment is but one part of this approach. Tractables must also be given (upon release) reintegrative assistance and therapeutic support.

Let us begin by considering the "safety net." A **safety net** is a group of individuals who have agreed to serve as problem solvers, role models, and advisers to a recently released inmate. These individuals provide transitional support to an offender as he/she reenters society. It is during this reentry stage that the ex-inmate is most in need of assistance. This net provides an ex-inmate with a group of trusted advocates. Thus, the offender may feel quite comfortable in seeking assistance from its members. Furthermore, the greater the net's "breadth" (referring to the total number of individuals who have agreed to assist an inmate) and the more frequent the contact between these individuals and the ex-inmate, the more likely it is that the offender will receive the assistance that he/she needs. The support provided by this "cooperative" will benefit the inmate by minimizing reintegrative shock. My experience suggests that those individuals who are especially helpful in this process include, but are not limited to, an inmate's

- family (both immediate and extended, to include a spouse, parents, and siblings),
- friends,
- neighbors,
- teachers,
- religious leaders or counselors, and
- employers.

While the development and use of "safety nets" for parolees would logically benefit both the ex-inmate and society, they remain largely unused within the contemporary correctional setting. I have met a few progressive officials who occasionally use them when confronted with especially challenging cases—but, overall, inmates are being returned to society with absolutely no transitional support from the community. In fact, community corrections officials frequently hear complaints from parolees about the difficulties they encounter in the absence of an active support system. Is it any wonder that inmates find this transition especially difficult or that such a large percentage of them reoffend so quickly following release?

If we acknowledge the value of treatment and accept the logic behind the safety net, perhaps we can also agree that there is a need for a closer alliance between correctional institutions and community officials. This alliance would ensure continuity in treatment processes between what is provided to an inmate during incarceration and the treatment provided to him/her upon release. Continuity is especially important since prison specialization requires a customized approach to correctional intervention. Through the formation of these partnerships, parole officials would become cognizant of the nature of an inmate's institutional treatment plan as well as his/her progress. This would provide parole agents with greater insight into a particular inmate's needs. All too often prison and parole officials fail to recognize that they are working toward the same objective. Thus, communications occur infrequently. By increasing communications and the level of cooperation that exists between these two, continuity in treatment would improve. A cooperative approach that unites prison and parole efforts inherently acknowledges that just as

> criminality in a given case has ordinarily developed from a number of inter-related influences, so must a correctional program be of a varied nature and interrelated if it is to combat effectively those influences. That criminal behavior has multiple causes and that treatment must therefore be many sided is a fundamental fact. (*Handbook on Classification*, p. 4)

While we should acknowledge the complex nature of modern criminality and address it more comprehensively, we must also regretfully acknowledge that a portion of the inmate population is beyond reform due to temporary or congenital conditions. **Defective** inmates are those offenders who are unable to participate in treatment programs because of extenuating conditions. Such conditions include physical, mental, and emotional impediments. Since a "defective" designation involves medical and psychological determinations, appropriate professionals must be involved in the classification process. While this label may be perceived as condemnatory by some, it reflects the inmate's condition(s) and is not a personal judgment of the individual. This is an important distinction. Gill does not advocate pronouncing people defective—rather that we recognize that a portion of the inmate population is simply unable to appreciate or fully participate in rehabilitative programming. The label "defective" could easily be changed to "challenged," "handicapped," or perhaps even "special-needs." In an attempt to provide appropriate care and to ensure that defective inmates are protected from predation, Gill proposes that defective inmates be housed in "partly custodial, partly hospital, and partly educational" prisons (Gill, 1972, p. 118). In the event a defective inmate's condition was to improve, reclassification might become necessary.

After reviewing Gill's proposals concerning prison specialization it should be obvious that housing intractable, tractable, and defective inmates within the same correctional facility is improper, "yet most of our state prisons have been built on this kind of hodgepodge intermingling" (Gill, 1972, p. 118). Progressive penologists have long criticized practitioners for taking such an indiscriminate approach to prison operations. Consider the following observation. This observation was made over 50 years ago but undeniably recognizes the value of specialization:

> [N]ot all offenders needed all of the constructive services which were being developed. Not all required vocational training or academic education or psychiatric treatment. To attempt to give all prisoners all services would be impractical, both because facilities would be diluted to the point where intensive work could not be done with any, and second, because such a program would fail to meet the specific needs of individual prisoners. (*Handbook on Classification*, p. 1)

This observation correctly identifies a few of the historical problems associated with generalized institutional placement. These problems still plague the contemporary prison. For example, when treatment is provided it is still diluted to the point of ineffectiveness. To increase the prison's ability to promote public safety we must adopt specialization. This approach would enable today's correctional facilities to meet the "needs" and "security requirements" of the entire inmate population. More specifically, specialization would provide treatment only to those for whom treatment is most appropriate while eliminating the corrupting effects of the intractable inmate.

Observations and Limitations

To fully assess the merit of Gill's proposal, it becomes necessary to recognize several "areas of concern." When I write about "areas of concern," I am specifically referring to questions left unanswered by Gill in his original manuscripts. One of these concerns is the difficulty involved in determining an inmate's tractability based largely upon his/her own statements. Given that people may practice deception to avoid discomfort, it should come as no surprise that inmates might attempt to manipulate the classification process in an attempt to avoid the labels "intractable" or "defective." Why? Well, both of these designations would result in a style of incarceration that is best described as simple and secure—in other words, with few amenities. Since tractable inmates would enjoy a more normalized and comfortable prison environment, a large proportion of the inmate population might attempt to convince officials that they are tractable when in fact they are not. So to what degree should officials accept inmate statements as valid indicators of their interests and intent? Should these statements be accepted at face value or should officials approach them with a good deal of skepticism? Gill provides little direction with regard to this portion of the process, but it seems logical to consider other sources of information including direct observation. Observations of an inmate's behavior while housed at an RDC would yield insight not available through a consideration of personal statements. Since the initial evaluation of new inmates will take several weeks, reception and diagnostic staff will become familiar with each inmate. This familiarity will prove crucial for accurate classification. While inmate statements and staff observations are useful, they provide limited insight. This is why interviews with an inmate's family, friends, and past employers become so important. While you may initially believe that these individuals would be hesitant to communicate with corrections officials, they are often willing to provide a degree of insight into the inmate's personality and background that is unavailable elsewhere. If steps are undertaken toward specialization, interviews of this kind will become such a vital part of this process that each RDC will utilize a special investigative unit. While statements, observations, and interviews appear to be the best methods available to determine tractability, the significance assigned to each of these approaches must be determined. Should each of these sources of information be given equal consideration or should one of them be weighed more heavily? Regardless of your thoughts about which method should be weighed more heavily or which should be discounted, every effort must be made to ensure that classification assessments are based upon multiple sources of information—anything less would compromise the integrity of this process.

Gill also maintains that once an inmate has made substantial progress toward reform further incarceration becomes unnecessary. Gill sees little value in prolonging a tractable inmate's term of incarceration beyond what is necessary to achieve a reformed state. It appears that Gill advocates this approach as a way to

- reduce correctional costs,
- minimize the effects of institutionalization,
- reduce the burden of incarceration upon the families of inmates, and
- facilitate reform.

This portion of Gill's proposal would require that we transform our sentencing structure from a determinate or fixed sentencing model to one that is based on indeterminate sentencing. **Determinate sentencing,** the model currently used in the United States, provides for a "fixed or specified" term of incarceration. For example, a judge might state that the defendant is sentenced to five years in the state prison. While it appears that the offender will serve a full five years in prison, many states have implemented some type of "mandatory parole." Under this approach, inmates with a pattern of clear conduct (clear conduct denotes compliance with institutional rules and staff directives) are normally released after serving about 50 percent of their sentence. Thus, in this example, the inmate would be paroled after serving two-and-a-half years. Furthermore, mandatory parole requires that this inmate's release be made without any consideration of how it might affect community safety. In an opposite fashion, **indeterminate sentencing,** the model that is endorsed by Gill and that was used nationwide until the mid-1970s, provides for a sentence range. For example, the judge under an indeterminate approach might sentence the defendant to a period of two-and-a-half to five years in the state prison. The inmate in this example is required to spend at least two-and-a-half years in prison, with a possibility for parole prior to the conclusion of the fifth year. Under an indeterminate approach, parole is granted only when an inmate has demonstrated clear conduct, has made substantial progress toward reform, and is able to convince corrections officials that he/she poses little or no danger to the community. The primary goal of indeterminate sentencing is to provide the tractable inmate with an incentive to use his/her term of confinement in a constructive manner. While it has now been about three decades since indeterminate sentencing was replaced with the determinate model, most citizens recognize its value as a mechanism to increase public safety. In addition to facilitating inmate reform, this approach empowers prison officials with the ability to retain those inmates who clearly present a substantial risk to society. Of course, a term of incarceration cannot exceed the upper limit set by the sentencing judge. In this sense, prison specialization is tough on the intractable inmate but attentive to those who sincerely desire reform.

How would substantial progress be determined? Any determination about progress would be based upon personal statements, observation, and interviews with treatment and security staff. While no process is infallible, decisions would be based on the best information available. You should have noticed by now that what is really being proposed is an infusion of discretion into the contemporary correctional process. The reason indeterminate sentencing was originally abandoned in the 1970s was a concern about the misuse of discretion by corrections officials. This is a legitimate concern and, of course, safeguards should be implemented to ensure fair and unbiased decisions. But when a system deals with an individual, it must fully understand that the needs and challenges being confronted necessitate an approach that is adaptable to the circumstances. It is only through the proper use of discretion that reform can be achieved and community safety increased. I make this observation based upon personal experience. While I was with the New Mexico Department of Corrections (a system that has mandatory parole), inmates who were aggressive, violent, and still held leadership positions in street gangs (and took a great deal of pride in doing so) were released without concern for public safety. Prison officials were powerless to stop this practice since determinate sentencing mandated these releases. Needless to say, many of these individuals reoffended and were quickly returned to the state prison system. Indeterminate sentencing would provide officials with the discretion needed to deal with these situations.

When speaking of specialized prisons, Gill also discounts the role that uniformed staff might conceivably play in treatment processes. Gill asserts that since uniformed staff are enforcers of institutional rules, they are naturally disassociated from reform initiatives. Such a belief is unfortunate since penologists have long known that offenders tend to have little respect for authority. By involving uniformed staff in the treatment process, a healthy respect for authority might be cultivated through open communication and positive interaction. Communication and interaction that is undertaken to aid an inmate directly may reduce misconceptions that an inmate holds with regard to those in authority. By humanizing "authority," inmates may also learn to respect the inherent legitimacy of the law. Similarly, others have recognized that the officer is "[is] in constant contact with the inmate and probably [has] the most influence on his attitudes and behavior" (*Handbook on Classification*, p. 8).

As this passage observes, security staff have more contact with the inmate population than do treatment personnel. Security staff are involved in every aspect of an inmate's daily life. This includes waking inmates for morning count, supervising work and educational assignments, ensuring that each inmate keeps his/her cell clean and organized, and overseeing meals and mail distribution. This contact provides an opportunity for involvement with the inmate population that goes far beyond what treatment personnel normally experience. To properly prepare tractables for release it would stand to reason that security personnel must become an extension of the treatment effort—making treatment initiatives part of the inmate's daily routine. Yes, security's primary mission must always be the production of a safe and orderly prison, but the purpose of institutional security should be broadened in those prisons housing tractable inmates. It is only through a cooperative approach that unites treatment and security efforts that the prison will ever become an environment that is conducive to inmate reform.

Summary

Ultimately the value of prison specialization can be found in its ability to increase public safety. The challenge remains as it has been for many years for penologists to convince practitioners that institutional reform can reduce recidivism rates. While Gill provides a general outline for prison specialization, he leaves many of the details to others. I believe that he chose to leave these details as a way to encourage discussion and debate. Furthermore, he was probably aware that such a proposal would not be immediately implemented, making detail unnecessary. I have reviewed Gill's ideas and believe them to be sound and obtainable. Having come from a correctional background, I can attest to the value of linking an inmate's amenability to his/her classification status. Responsible classification processes require us to separate inmates based upon tractability and to provide treatment only to those who are most likely to benefit. Such an approach would reduce both operating costs and recidivism rates. Furthermore, by returning to an indeterminate sentencing model, the correctional system would regain the discretion that it needs to effectively deal with the contemporary offender. It is only through a return to indeterminate sentencing that inmates will be given an incentive to seek reform. Likewise, indeterminate sentencing will enable prison officials to retain those offenders who present a "clear and present" danger to society. As you ponder prison specialization, consider how it might be advanced through the increasingly popular practice of prison privatization. Privatization is the topic of the next chapter.

Chapter Highlights

1. There are two groups of inmates—those who are tractable and those who are not.
2. Many of today's correctional professionals find it difficult to identify the traditional goals of the prison.
3. The original purpose of inmate classification was to diagnose an inmate's needs then design an appropriate course of treatment to meet those needs.
4. Classification based upon a consideration of both treatment and security concerns is essential if a prison is to maximize its social value.
5. Under the Pennsylvania system inmates were completely isolated from one another and produced small craft-related items.
6. Under the Auburn system inmates congregated for work and built large industrial items, including boilers, machinery, and engines.
7. Since the Auburn system permitted congregate labor, it proved more financially profitable than did the Pennsylvania system.
8. Normalization provides inmates with a wide range of treatment choices and promotes responsible behavior.

9. Generalized incarceration refers to the practice of housing intractable, tractable, and defective inmates in the same facility, thereby permitting them to interact with each other.
10. If an inmate is "new," he/she is awaiting initial classification and institutional placement.
11. Intractable inmates refuse to participate in treatment initiatives.
12. Tractable inmates are interested in treatment and reform.
13. "Defective" inmates are unable to participate in treatment due to a condition that renders participation impossible.
14. The contemporary prison is simply the best "college of crime" available to the offender.
15. Custodial prisons are institutions where security and orderly operations are pursued to the exclusion of all other objectives
16. While progressive prisons offer treatment and educational initiatives, these programs are underfunded, understaffed, and tend to serve as "management tools" rather than mechanisms of reform.
17. Professional prisons seek to facilitate inmate reform by providing high-quality treatment programs that employ well-qualified staff.
18. Offender treatment may begin in the prison but must continue once an inmate is paroled.
19. Treatment and security should be viewed as interrelated activities that share a common objective—the long-term safety of society.
20. Determinate sentencing provides for a fixed term of incarceration (e.g., five years, of which the inmate will usually serve two-and-a-half years).
21. Indeterminate sentencing provides for a sentence range (e.g., two-and-a-half to five years). In this example, an inmate could be paroled after as little as two-and-a-half years or might be required to serve the entire sentence in prison.
22. Indeterminate sentencing is closely related to rehabilitative ideology since it links parole to an inmate's progress toward reform.

Discussion Questions

1. Should inmates be thought of as being "tractable" or "intractable"? Why?
2. What are the advantages and disadvantages of separating inmates based upon perceived reformability?
3. Are there difficulties associated with determining an inmate's suitability for treatment? If so, name a few?

4. Are other sources of information available (in addition to personal statements, interviews, and observations) that would help officials determine an inmate's suitability for treatment? If so, what are they and would acquiring this information be feasible?

5. Has rehabilitation as a correctional objective outlived its usefulness? If so, what objective should take its place?

6. What are the primary differences between intractable and defective inmates?

7. Why did the Pennsylvania approach to prison management fail? Was its use of isolation conducive to reform? Explain.

8. What are the characteristics of custodial, progressive, and professional prisons?

9. What are the objectives of the initial classification committee? How do its objectives differ from those of the reclassification committee?

10. Can an intractable inmate become tractable? Explain.

11. What is a "safety net" and why is it important to both a parolee and the community?

12. Which is more conducive to inmate reform—determinate or indeterminate sentencing? Why?

13. How can security staff promote inmate reform? How can treatment personnel promote institutional security?

Sources

Gill, H. 1962. Correctional Philosophy and Architecture. *Journal of Criminal Law, Criminology and Police Science*, 53 (3), pp. 312–322; reprinted in R. Carter, D. Glaser, and Leslie Wilkins, eds. *Correctional Institutions*. New York: J. B. Lippincott Company.

Handbook on Classification in Correctional Institutions. 1965. Philadelphia, PA: The American Foundation—Studies in Corrections.

Jarvis, Dwight. 1978. *Institutional Treatment of the Offender*. New York: McGraw-Hill Publishing.

If prison specialization becomes a reality, it may well be the private prison that houses and reforms tractable inmates.

Chapter Four

Prison Privatization

I include a chapter on prison privatization since anecdotal evidence suggests that the private sector will play a significant role in the future of America's prison system, especially if prison specialization is adopted. The full extent to which the private sector will become involved in prison operations is yet to be seen. However, by considering contemporary perceptions related to prison privatization, we can reasonably estimate the degree of influence that it will exert on future correctional operations. Perceptions that prove especially enlightening can be obtained from those with a unique insight into this phenomenon. While numerous groups may possess this insight, there are just two that are appropriate for our consideration—the nation's judicial officials, who are eminently knowledgeable about prison conditions and inmate treatment, and print journalists, who are knowledgeable about social movements and public policy issues. These two groups frequently comment on contemporary issues and are featured on such popular and long-running television programs as *Meet the Press* and *Washington Journal*. In addition to the unique relationship that members of these two groups have with the prison, they also produce documentation appropriate for scholarly review.

By considering the information and insight that judicial records and news-paper articles offer, we can learn a great deal about the growing trend to privatize prisons. Prison privatization is of immense importance since it may well be the private prison that shoulders the formidable responsibility for housing and reforming the tractable inmate in the future.

> *What if . . . you were asked to visualize a "typical" prison? Would your mental image be negative or positive? Why?*

Why Prison Privatization?

With growing demands for prison space outpacing the government's ability to construct additional prisons, many jurisdictions have begun to look to the private sector for solutions. The private sector, unlike its public counterpart, is often able to build and staff prisons quickly and without the restrictive red tape that slows conventional processes. **Prison privatization** specifically refers to the process whereby the government contracts with a private corporation for the construction and operation of correctional facilities. The private sector is willing to construct and operate prisons if it is financially profitable to do so. Profit margins are often determined by contract length and the per diem fee negotiated between the parties. **Per diem** refers to the daily fee that the government pays a private operator to house inmates on its behalf. This fee can approach $75.00 per day per inmate, but is often much less. While figures vary slightly, about 10 percent of the total U.S. prisoner population is now incarcerated in privately operated prisons. Global figures, although incomplete, reveal that incarceration in privately operated prisons is becoming popular in Europe, Australia, and South Africa.

While a shortage of prison space is helping drive contemporary prison privatization, privatization's roots can be traced to the 1960s, when social dissent was spreading throughout the United States. It was then that Americans began to question their place in society and the failure of the government to respect the constitutional rights of all citizens. It was increasingly recognized that the "American dream" was closed to a large percentage of the population. This resulted in frustration and a growing belief that civil disobedience would be necessary if changes were to be brought about. The trigger for this action was the **Vietnam War**. This war, opposed by a large segment of society, served to polarize American youth (the segment of the population most affected by the war), who increasingly began to mobilize themselves in protest; other groups comprised women, students, and inmates, all of whom sought to politicize their own agenda. Each group questioned the role of the government in society. Marches, sit-ins, boycotts, rallies, and demonstrations of all kinds became common. With growing social dissatisfaction, the government's traditional monopoly over public services was openly criticized. Citizens realized that the government was unable to provide a number of services on the scale or of the quality that they demanded. This forced politicians to consider privatizing a number of traditional governmental operations, including those associated with the prison.

Besides overcrowding and widespread dissatisfaction with the government, other factors that have contributed to the prison privatization movement include

- an ongoing shortage of public funding for the expansion and construction of prisons,
- the perception that the private sector is able to build and staff prisons more quickly and cheaply than can government jurisdictions,
- a general movement worldwide to reduce the size of government, and
- a realization that the private sector has historically provided a number of high-quality and low-cost services to the government.

The government's role in the apprehension, prosecution, and punishment of the offender is a relatively recent development. In fact, for the most part of human history, the protection of life and property was a private matter. English law, from which American law evolved, derived many of its practices from **Anglo-Saxon** custom, under which individuals living in small kindred and tribal groups relied on group solidarity for protection. It was the citizenry who enforced shared ideals of justice. Offenders were often required to pay restitution. The amount of restitution was set by custom and was collected by the victim or his/her family. Later, those with political power became increasingly involved in this process. Eventually, all crimes became offenses against the established political leader and were no longer viewed as offenses against commoners. This made the collection of fines and confiscated properties a political pursuit that was financially profitable for the government.

Given that the private pursuit of justice was the norm for the most part of human history, it should come as no surprise that early European prisons were privately operated. The operators sought profit by charging fees for admittance and discharge as well as for food and water. Many of the ideologies common in Europe were also brought to the New World. Without an infrastructure specifically designed to process offenders, colonial justice depended on direct citizen participation. **Jeremy Bentham** (an early nineteenth-century English correctional philosopher) advocated the use of large circular prisons called **panopticons**. These types of prisons, designed to allow officials to keep inmates under constant surveillance, were originally intended to be privately operated. The panopticon's design was adopted in America and influenced prison construction well into the early twentieth century. The most famous panopticon-style prison still in existence today is run by the State of Illinois and is commonly called **Stateville Penitentiary** (1916), but is officially designated the Stateville Correctional Center. As colonial society became increasingly more complex, a rudimentary criminal justice system emerged. The emergence of this system made the pursuit and punishment of the offender a governmental responsibility and not the responsibility of private parties. Private involvement in prison affairs was eventually pushed to the periphery of penal operations. Once lodged there, the private sector provided educational, kitchen, and laundry services.

Though the groundwork for prison privatization can be traced to early European practices and then to a reemerging interest in it during the 1960s, it was ónly in the mid-1980s that local governmental jurisdictions in **Tennessee** and **Florida** actually began to experiment with jail privatization. However, to **Kentucky** goes the distinction of being the first state to partially privatize its prison system. Currently, there are an estimated 158 private correctional facilities operating in 31 states.

Table 4.1 outlines a number of characteristics associated with both the public and private prison sectors.

As table 4.1 reveals, there are a number of characteristics that highlight the similarities and differences between publicly and privately operated prisons. Few differences exist between the racial and gender make-up of either sector's inmate populations or the average age at admission. However, when we consider the average number of months served by each sector's inmates, we do see significant differences. The average term of incarceration served by inmates in public prisons is more than twice that served by private sector inmates. This is a direct result of the security level at which each sector's prisons operate. For example, the public sector has about 70 percent of its prisons operating at the medium- and minimum-security levels, with a large percentage of its prisons operating at maximum security. In contrast, the private sector has about 90 percent of its prisons operating at the medium- or minimum-security levels, with over half of these being minimum-security institutions. Thus, the private

TABLE 4.1. Select Characteristics of Public and Private Prisons

	Public	**Private**
Inmate		
Race		
African American (%)	47	43
White (%)	43	32
Other/unknown (%)	10	25
Gender		
Male (%)	94	90
Female (%)	6	10
Age at admission (years)	31	30
Average length of stay (months)	28	11
Employee		
Officer salary		
Minimum ($)	21,855	19,344
Maximum ($)	34,728	21,790
Preservice training (hours)	240	177
Institution		
Custody levels*		
Maximum (%)	27	6
Medium (%)	37	43
Minimum (%)	32	47

*Due to the exclusion of small temporary holding facilities for which data are largely unavailable, custody figures total 96 percent.

sector specializes in housing the less serious and the less hardened offender, while the public sector tends to retain the more serious and dangerous offender. The private sector prefers to operate lower-security prisons because

- they are less expensive to build,
- they require fewer security personnel,
- the staff command lower wages,
- the staff can be more easily recruited, and
- housing the less serious inmate produces little or no public opposition.

The public sector retains high-security inmates because government officials

- remain uncertain about the private sector's ability to house dangerous inmates,
- remain uncertain about the civil liability associated with placing high-risk inmates into privately operated prisons,
- are aware that the citizenry is not yet comfortable with having the private sector house dangerous inmates, and
- wish to maintain a niche for themselves, thereby ensuring the government's continuing role.

When reviewing the sector characteristics detailed in table 4.1, it becomes apparent that the private sector is undertaking measures to minimize operating costs and increase profit margins (i.e., employee pay and training figures). Since prison privatization is based upon a profit rationale, opponents of privatization have expressed concern about the relationship that is developing between private operators and government officials. They are quick to accuse the private sector of attempting to increase its profit margins by involving itself in political processes; they claim that the private sector may even lobby for the increased use of incarceration as a criminal sanction. While these concerns remain little more than speculation, a brief consideration of the relationship that is developing between the private sector and government officials may provide insight into the private sector's role in future prison operations.

Privatization and Politics

A general consensus exists among social scientists that a movement is afoot globally to privatize traditional governmental services. Many of these services relate to education and the provision of utilities and transportation. A proposal to privatize the entire U.S. social security system has been gaining momentum for some time now. While corporations profit from the partnerships that are being forged between the public and private sectors, the process enables governments to meet the demands on their finite resources and expertise. Since profit is involved, the private sector naturally seeks additional opportunities for financial gain. It is no wonder then that the private sector desires increased privatization of government services. This objective necessitates the cultivation of ties to political leadership, which in turn help ensure that corporate interests are considered during the awarding of contracts and during legislative undertakings. One of the most effective ways for the private sector to curry favor with public officials is through campaign contributions. Both President Bush and former presidential candidate Al Gore accepted substantial contributions from the private prison sector during their bid for office. These campaign contributions are intended to cultivate a positive relationship between the sectors. This practice is ingrained in American political history and dates to the beginning of our political system.

> *What if . . . you were to learn that the private prison sector frequently makes campaign contributions? Would you be concerned? Why?*

Corporations also seek expansion by funding university-based research. For example, institutions of higher education are increasingly receiving corporate support. Since 1981, corporate funding to U.S. universities alone has increased fivefold. While data are unavailable on the extent of similar activities by the private prison sector, there is evidence to suggest that they are occurring. For example, not much has been written about Professor Charles Thomas, a tenured professor at the University of Florida and arguably the world's leading scholar on prison privatization. His research appeared frequently in academic journals and lent credibility to the pro-privatization movement. It was due in part to Thomas's reputation and endorsement that many jurisdictions privatized their correctional facilities. Few were aware, however, that private operators had invested a substantial amount of money in Thomas's research. Though each of the parties involved denied impropriety, questions lingered about this relationship. Ethical questions aside, Thomas and others have promoted prison privatization by asserting that

- private operators are more likely to adhere to civil rights and due process protections than are public operators since judicial judgments would threaten profit margins,
- privatization leads to increased operational efficiency by reducing wasteful practices, and
- the private sector is able to recruit employees with greater levels of expertise and experience than are usually accessible to the public sector.

Opponents of privatization frequently claim that

- the private sector seeks profit at the expense of civil rights protections,
- privatization negatively affects inmate reform since a financial incentive exists to reduce treatment, counseling, and educational and recreational programming, and
- the private sector employs a less qualified and more transient workforce primarily because it offers lower wages.

All indications suggest that the private sector is interested in assuming a more prominent role in prison operations. This desire is not only reflected in corporate mission statements, but also becomes apparent when private sector involvement in political processes and in the sponsorship of prison-related research is considered. The ongoing debate about the advantages and disadvantages of prison privatization suggests that much remains to be learnt about this approach. It is this uncertainty about privatization that continues to provide fertile ground for debate and speculation. Debate and speculation warrant greater attention being paid to the perceptions of our judges and journalists, which are certain to influence future prison operations and help determine the level of public support that privatization will receive. A better understanding of these perceptions will also help us determine how best to utilize the attributes of the private sector to increase public safety and facilitate prison specialization.

The Approach

To acquire insight into prison privatization, content analysis was conducted on lawsuits in which inmates alleged violations of their constitutional rights. **Content analysis** is a method by which communications, both written and spoken, are analyzed to determine how a group perceives an issue and how these perceptions are communicated to a larger audience. Content analysis permits a determination to be made about the level of support a practice is receiving and the overall manner in which it is portrayed to the general citizenry. Lawsuits represent the best source of data available on judicial sentiment regarding privatization. Furthermore, lawsuits reveal a great deal of information about the private prison sector. By considering judicial statements, a better understanding of privatization's effects on the prison can be obtained. **Title 42 Sec. 1983** is currently the predominant act by which inmates seek federal judicial intervention. This act reads (in part):

> Every person who, under color of any statute, ordinance, regulation, custom, or usage, of any State or Territory of the District of Columbia, subjects, or causes to be subjected, any citizen of the United States or other person within the jurisdiction thereof to the deprivation of any rights, privileges, or immunities secured by the Constitution and laws, shall be liable to the party injured in an action of law, suit in equity, or other proper proceeding for redress . . .

To begin the content analysis, a search was conducted to locate Title 42 Sec. 1983 suits filed against the private sector. This search revealed 140 suits, of which 108 were determined to be unsuitable for complete analysis. Many of these were filed against a jail and not a prison operator. Thus, 32 suits filed against the private sector were selected for analysis. A search for a comparable sample of suits filed against publicly operated prisons was also conducted. This resulted in the selection of 32 suits, of which 15 were determined to be unusable. Many of these were either filed against a jail and not a prison operator or did not raise issues specifically covered under Title 42 Sec. 1983. Finally 17 public suits were selected. Thus a total of 49 suits were chosen for the analysis.

A search for newspaper articles dealing with prisons and prison privatization revealed that 2,654 articles had been published between

1986 (the approximate year that contemporary privatization began) and 2002. A total of 151 articles (approximately a 17 percent sample) was then randomly selected for consideration. Of these, 22 were determined to be inappropriate for analysis since they tended to make only a passing mention of prison privatization or were so broad in scope as to mislead the reader. For example, one article dealt with a kidnapper who had created his own private prison in an underground shelter. Thus, 129 articles were chosen for analysis.

Statements made by inmates or their representatives appearing in legal documents and newspaper articles were excluded from analysis, since those statements had the potential to be biased and misleading. Only statements made by judges and journalists (or their interviewees) were considered. In some articles, journalists paraphrased inmate statements to lend credibility to their positions. When this occurred, the statements were considered to a limited extent, since they were ancillary to the overall nature of the article. No consideration was given to the final outcome of lawsuits, since judicial decisions often involve decrees and negotiated settlements that do not necessarily assign fault. Furthermore, the advantages and disadvantages associated with both privatization and traditional government operations are manifest within judicial statements themselves, making a consideration of the suit's final outcome irrelevant. The content and manner in which issues were presented in both lawsuits and print were determined to portray privatization in a favorable, neutral, or unfavorable fashion. A favorable presentation refers to those statements that are complimentary to privatization. A neutral presentation refers to those suits or articles whose presentation had both favorable and unfavorable language in equal measure. An unfavorable presentation refers to those suits or articles that present privatization as a negative practice. Since neutral statements yield little substantive insight into privatization, judicial excerpts appearing in this chapter are limited to those of a favorable or unfavorable nature.

Findings: An Overview of Allegations

Interestingly enough, when considering those suits filed against the private sector, half alleged a violation of due process procedures

TABLE 4.2. Percentage of Lawsuits in Which Allegations Appeared

Violation type	Private sector	Public sector
Due process	50	40
Medical treatment	40	50
Physical security	25	33
Cruel/unusual punishment	25	20
Denial of religious freedoms	20	—
Denial of court access	20	33
Abuse and harassment	17	6
Living conditions	—	10
Physical conditions	3	—

Note: These are approximations rounded to the nearest percentage point.

(see table 4.2). These allegations frequently claimed that inmates were unfairly segregated, improperly transferred, improperly disciplined, or denied free speech. **Due process** refers to a set of legal procedures that provide an inmate the opportunity to challenge institutional decisions that place unreasonable restrictions on rights or that adversely affect placement or programming. In about four of every ten suits, allegations pertained to **medical treatment,** including the withholding of medication or medical procedures. It appeared that allegations of this nature were considered to be especially significant by the judiciary, since they carried the potential to have an immediate as well as lasting effect upon the inmate's health. In a quarter of the suits, allegations pertained to physical security. **Physical security** denotes the use of excessive force by prison personnel to enforce institutional rules or staff orders, failure to protect an inmate from assault, failure to protect inmate property from destruction or theft, or negligent supervision that directly places inmates at grave risk of serious bodily injury. In a quarter of the suits, inmate allegations pertained to **cruel and unusual punishments,** denoting treatment that is unconstitutional or is recognized as unacceptable. Often, cruel and unusual punishments were cited along with other allegations in an attempt to stress the harmful nature of the acts being alleged. In about a fifth of the suits, allegations related to **denial of religious freedoms,** including expression and assembly. In slightly less than a fifth of the suits, allegations related to denial of court access. **Denial of court access** refers to impeding an inmate's ability to file judicial paperwork or to send or receive legal communications.

Allegations of abuse and harassment by prison officials were cited in about a sixth of the private sector suits. **Abuse and harassment** refers to staff actions and statements intended to create fear or distress. Finally, allegations pertaining to physical conditions were cited in about 3 percent of the suits. **Physical conditions** pertain to the overall nature of confinement, including overcrowding, inadequate sanitation, exposure to excessive and constant noise, and exposure to environmental toxins.

When considering suits filed against the public sector, four of every ten contained allegations of due process violation. Slightly more than half related to medical treatment. In about a third of these suits, allegations related to denial of court access. A third mentioned physical security, with about a fifth citing cruel and unusual punishments. In just over a tenth of the suits, allegations related to **living conditions**. Claims of unconstitutional actions associated with living conditions mentioned inadequate diet and the lack of opportunity for exercise. Of the suits considered, 6 percent involved allegations pertaining to abuse and harassment.

Overall, allegations related mainly to due process, cruel and unusual punishments, and religious freedoms. Abuse and harassment were more prevalent in suits filed against the private sector than in suits filed against the government. While a consideration of allegation frequency is insightful, a consideration of the context in which these allegations appeared yields even greater insight. This consideration also provides some indication as to the general level of support that the judiciary gives to prison privatization. Specific operational subjects that emerged from a review of these suits include inmate safety, prison management, conflict resolution, profit, race (as well as ethnicity and gender), staff training, and recreation.

Context of Operational Issues

Inmate Safety

Though in a third of the lawsuits filed against the private sector inmate safety was mentioned, a majority of these had the presiding judge writing of safety in a neutral manner. The three suits in which judges presented inmate safety in an unfavorable fashion dealt with inmate abuse, the withholding of medical care, and an inmate's murder; presiding judges found both operators to have disregarded inmate safety. In the suit involving murder, the court recognized that improper classification procedures (see chapter 3) resulted in the mixing of maximum- and medium-security inmates, creating an unsafe correctional setting (*Scott v. District of Columbia*, 1999). In this incident, a maximum-security inmate known to be violent attacked and killed an inmate with a lower-security rating. It goes without saying that both these inmates were housed in the same institution. This suit raised questions related to generalized institutional placement and clearly illustrated the need for appropriate classification procedures.

In about four of every ten suits filed against the public sector, presiding judges mentioned safety in a neutral manner. In no suit filed against the public sector was safety mentioned favorably or unfavorably. Thus, while judges mentioned inmate safety in connection with the private sector in both neutral and unfavorable contexts, in the public sector suits, it appeared only in a neutral context.

Prison Management

Judges mentioned prison management in about a tenth of the suits filed against private operators (once favorably and twice unfavorably). Prison management as it appeared in these suits pertained to administrative practices that allegedly created an environment conducive to civil rights infringements. The suit in which judicial statements appeared favorable to privatization involved inmate abuse, inadequate medical treatment, and denial of religious freedoms. Although this suit involved multiple allegations, the presiding judge concluded that the administrative pursuit of profit (a defining feature of the private sector) is unlikely to lead to prison mismanagement or inmate abuse. This finding challenges claims by opponents of privatization that the private sector will circumvent constitutional protections or established operational protocol to reduce expenditures and increase profit. The court further stated that "squeezing profits out of violations of constitutional rights would be a tricky path to navigate at best" (*Citrano v. Allen Correctional Center*, 1995).

In the first suit where a judge mentioned prison management in an unfavorable context, allegations pertained to the physical abuse of dozens of inmates. It was further shown that this particular private operator had knowingly hired correctional officers with previous convictions for "prisoner abuse" at a public sector prison. The employment of these individuals was considered by the judiciary as significantly contributing to the creation of an unsafe and hostile correctional environment. In the second suit where prison management was mentioned unfavorably, an inmate with a security classification of medium was attacked and killed by a maximum-security inmate known to be extremely violent. In fact, this maximum-security inmate had committed numerous similar attacks in the past. The interesting part of this suit is that both the contracting jurisdiction and the private operator violated classification procedures and chose to mix highly dangerous inmates with those who were docile and easily victimized (*Scott v. District of Columbia*, 1999). In both these suits, the presiding judges found the management practices of the private sector responsible for the creation of an environment conducive to civil rights infringements.

In no suit filed against the government was prison mismanagement mentioned.

Conflict Resolution

One way to assess a prison administration's willingness and ability to properly manage its facilities is to consider its efforts to resolve conflict at an early stage. Effective resolution requires not only suitable remedies, but also the implementation of safeguards to ensure that similar injuries do not reoccur. **Grievance procedures** specifically refer to processes that provide inmates an opportunity to resolve disputes outside the judicial arena. Methods of resolving disputes through institutional grievance processes were specifically mentioned by judges in slightly less than a quarter of those suits filed against the private sector. While in a majority of these suits, judicial statements were neutral, in one they were unfavorable. In the suit where grievances were mentioned unfavorably, inmates claimed that a multitude of complaints had been filed over one specific incident. Nonetheless, this prison's administration openly refused to conduct an investigation. Even more interesting is the court's finding that the institutional grievance officer arbitrarily discarded many of these complaints by disposing of them in the trash. The presiding judge found this especially shocking since formalized grievance procedures are required by the U.S. Supreme Court's ruling in *Jones v. North Carolina Prisoner's Labor Union* (1977). Furthermore, administrators universally recognize grievance procedures as essential to the safe and orderly operation of correctional institutions. Without the ability to register a concern about a particular event or practice, inmates become frustrated and they may resort to violence as a way to voice dissent (see the discussion of the Attica and Santa Fe riots, chapter 2). Grievance procedures specifically stipulate a mandatory investigation, the publication of the investigation findings, and an opportunity for aggrieved inmates to appeal. The judge in this particular case recognized that "grievances filed in every single instance . . . produced no response" *(Kesler et al. v. Brazoria County, 1998)*.

Judges mentioned conflict resolution in a neutral context in about seven out of every ten public sector suits.

Profit

Judges mentioned profit in about a fifth of the lawsuits filed against the private sector. In slightly more than one-half of these, judicial statements were neutral. Of the three suits in which judicial statements portrayed profit unfavorably, two pertained to withholding necessary medical services, while the last one involved a failure by prison authorities to provide employees with adequate training: staff training was allegedly reduced or withheld as a way to decrease operating expenditures. In each of these suits, the court spoke quite sternly to the private sector and linked the pursuit of profit to civil rights violations, inmate mistreatment, and cost-cutting practices (*McKnight v. Rees*, 1996; *Bowman v. Corrections Corporation of America et al.*, 2000; *Kesler et al. v. Brazoria County*, 1998).

Profit was mentioned neutrally in one public sector suit in which the court found no evidence to substantiate an inmate's claim that a public official was misappropriating prison funds for personal benefit (*West v. Keating*, 2001).

Race, Ethnicity, and Gender

Judges mentioned race, ethnicity, and gender neutrally in a tenth of the suits filed against the private sector. These suits were quite diverse in nature and involved the alleged rape of a female inmate by a male correctional officer, an anti-Semitic slur, racial tensions between African American and Caucasian inmates, and the strip searching of male inmates by female officers.

Race was neutrally mentioned in one public suit involving an African American inmate who claimed he was being underpaid in comparison with a white clerk (*Perry v. Rose et al.,* 2000). The presiding judge found no merit in this allegation and dismissed the suit as frivolous.

Staff Training

Staff training was mentioned in about a tenth of the suits filed against the private sector. Staff training commonly takes one of two forms. The first is **preservice** training. Preservice training is provided to fresh employees to familiarize them with their new duties and responsibilities and is completed before their initial assignment. Most prison systems require correctional officer cadets to complete approximately 240 hours of preservice training. In contrast, **in-service** training is provided on an ongoing basis and is generally required as a condition of continued employment. Most prison systems require regular employees to complete approximately 40 hours of in-service training every year. The primary difference between these two forms of training is that while preservice is designed to prepare an individual for employment, inservice is designed to ensure that the seasoned employee remains competent. In three suits filed against the private sector, judicial commentary about staff training was neutral; in one, the commentary was unfavorable. In this suit, the court stated that it was "satisfied that the violent and humiliating events of that evening were substantially and causally related to the lack of training" (*Kesler et al. v. Brazoria County,* 1998).

In no lawsuit filed against the public sector was staff training mentioned.

Recreation

Recreation refers to those activities that promote an inmate's physical and mental well-being. Common recreational activities found in prisons include weight lifting, basketball, baseball, racquetball, and boxing. Recreational activities also include board games, video games, and a host of craft-related hobbies. While recreational activity was not mentioned in litigation filed against the private sector, it was mentioned in a neutral context in conjunction with the placement of an inmate into disciplinary housing in one suit filed against the public sector. **Disciplinary housing** refers to the area of a prison that is reserved for inmates who are being punished for violating institutional rules. Inmates in disciplinary housing are segregated from other inmates as both a punitive measure and as a means to ensure the safety of other inmates. Disciplinary segregation also guards against further institutional disruption. The inmate who filed this particular suit claimed that he was maliciously denied an opportunity to participate in recreational exercises after he was moved to disciplinary housing (*Bridgeforth v. Ramsey et al.*, 1999). The judge found this case to be without merit.

Sector Comparisons Made by the Judiciary

It is especially interesting to note that the judiciary, in about 10 percent of the suits filed against the private sector, compared private employees with their public counterparts. In the first of these suits, the court concluded that immunity from civil liability, a protection traditionally reserved for public personnel, should also be extended to the private sector. This particular judge considered private and public prison staff to be functional equivalents. This position creates the possibility that similar protections will, at some future date, be extended to private sector employees (*Citrano and Chapman v. Allen Correctional Center*, 1995). In the second suit, the court compared the duties of private and public employees and concluded that the sectors shared more similarities than differences. However, the presiding judge, who did note an exception with employee training, found that the private sector's desire to minimize expenditure and maximize profit might contribute to reductions in staff training (*Kesler et al. v. Brazoria Country Sheriff King et al.*, 1998). While reductions in staff training might, at first glance, appear rather benign, the judge implied that they would lead to an overall degradation of the entire prison environment. In essence, an untrained staff would be less prepared to interact with the inmate population in a constitutional fashion than would a highly trained staff. In the last suit, the court similarly stated that when profit is introduced into prison operations, private employees are more likely to engage in activities based upon a financial motive than are their public counterparts (*McKnight v. Rees et al.*, 1996).

In no suit filed against a public operator were comparisons made with the private sector.

Portrayals of Prison Privatization by Print Journalists

In portrayals of prison privatization by print journalists, a pattern emerged in the level of support appearing within both article titles and article content. Overall, titles have become less favorable and more neutral since the 1980s, while article content has become more unfavorable. For example, during the 1980s, titles and content were favorable in slightly less than a fifth of the articles reviewed. However, by the early 2000s, favorable coverage had decreased significantly (see table 4.3).

Generally, unfavorable article titles tended to present prison privatization as a practice that frequently results in the mistreatment of the

TABLE 4.3. Nature of Article Content

Decade	Unfavorable (%)	Neutral (%)	Favorable (%)
1980s			
Title	33	50	17
Content	25	58	17
1990s			
Title	30	63	6
Content	37	56	7
2000s			
Title	35	61	4
Content	46	46	8

inmate population. These titles also suggested that the private sector is able to operate in a manner that is less accountable to the citizenry than is the public sector. A sample of phrases appearing in unfavorable titles include

state should continue to prohibit privately run prisons (*The Patriot-News*, Harrisburg, PA, 1987),

critics point to problems (*Tulsa World*, 1998),

state to probe alleged abuse (*Milwaukee Journal Sentinel*, 1998),

federal lawsuits allege guards tortured, violated civil rights (*Milwaukee Journal Sentinel*, 1999),

private prisons scoff at Florida law (*Palm Beach Post*–1997).

In favorable article titles, the journalistic focus was on the ability of the private sector to ease prison crowding and boost local economies through job creation. A sample of phrases appearing in favorable titles include

facilities may ease crowding (*Washington Post*, 1988),

town profits from prison (*Plain Dealer*, Cleveland, OH, 1995),

[officials] take steps to lure private prison to the county (*Virginian-Pilot*, Norfolk, VA, 1995).

In terms of unfavorable article content, journalists often suggested that a link exists between profit, prison mismanagement, and violence. A sample of these statements include

there is the possibility for the profit motive to be misused (Director of Nebraska's Department of Corrections, *Omaha World Herald*, 1986),

the profit motive may be placed ahead of service (*The Patriot-News*, Harrisburg, PA, 1987),

it sickens me (Rep. Ted Strickland [OH]) to think that individuals sit in corporate boardrooms talking about increasing their bottom line when the commodity they are dealing with is captive human lives (*Washington Post*, 1999),

the privatization experiment was marred by problems that included riots, and other violence (*Advocate*, 2000).

> *What if . . . you were a private operator? Would increased negativity in the print medium be a concern? What would you do to help reverse this trend?*

Favorable article content frequently referenced the successes experienced by the private sector in other jurisdictions. These accounts were used to endorse privatization by suggesting the probability of localized success. Journalists taking this position regularly portrayed the private sector as operating state-of-the-art prisons that are more technically advanced than those operated by the public sector. These prisons were also depicted as being more humane. For example,

> I think it ought to be tried, said Hobby (Lt. Governor of Texas). Apparently, they've had a good record in other states (*Houston Chronicle*, 1987).
>
> But inmates say privatization already has succeeded in other ways: The facility is cleaner and has better food and more humane conditions than any state prison they have experienced (*Austin American Statesman*, 1989).

Similar to judicial records, newspaper articles also contained specific themes. Well over half the articles that were reviewed dealt with some facet of overcrowding, with most journalists writing about this topic in a neutral fashion. Generally, journalists, while recognizing a need for additional prison space, neither supported nor challenged the private sector's ability to provide that space. Instead they portrayed the private sector's ability to provide additional space as a fact not open to judgment or interpretation. While approximately a fifth of the articles dealt with the issue of operational savings, about a third presented privatization as a cost-saving practice. Similarly, less than a fifth of the articles dealt with prison employees, and all of those portrayed privatization as having a negative effect on employee retention. Journalists implied that private sector employees are transitory in nature because of low training and low wage levels. Furthermore, a tenth of the articles pertained to grievance procedures, with a majority of the journalists taking a neutral position with regard to the private sector's willingness and ability to resolve conflict outside the judicial arena. The theme of due process protections appeared in about 3 percent of the articles, with one half of those portraying privatization as having a negative effect on these safeguards. Other themes are detailed in table 4.4.

TABLE 4.4. Themes Appearing in Newsprint

	Percentage of articles	Percentage of times mentioned		
		F	N	U
Prisons				
Capacity level	62	6	79	15
Overcrowding	24	7	74	19
Conditions	33	5	17	62
Savings	20	33	56	11
Profit	25	3	53	44
Profit's effects on civil rights	5	—	17	83
Violence	24	3	58	39
Safety	12	13	53	33
Staff				
Lawsuit	21	—	74	26
Wages	15	37	5	58
Training	9	—	36	64
Turnover	7	—	—	100
Inmate				
Treatment	16	19	62	—
Inmate grievances	10	—	85	15
Due process	3	—	50	50

Note: F = favorable; N = neutral; U = unfavorable.

Sector Comparisons Made by the Print Medium

In about a quarter of the articles reviewed, journalists compared the private and public sectors. In about half of these comparisons, journalists suggested that private prisons are more efficient than their public counterparts. In just over 2 percent of the articles, sector comparisons were made with regard to levels of institutional violence. Journalists appeared uncertain about any link that may exist between privatization and violence. They raised the possibility of such a relationship, but were apprehensive about making any definitive statement suggesting that the private sector experiences violence at a greater frequency than does the public sector. One of the most condemning observations concerning violence (even if it is relatively benign) appeared in the *Albuquerque Journal,* where it was observed that a private prison had experienced a greater level of violence than had nearby public facilities (1999). Overall, the media were less supportive of privatization than were judicial officials. For example, the print medium frequently portrayed profit as having a more negative effect on the civil rights of inmate populations than did the judiciary.

Common Beliefs Debunked

Many of the portrayals outlined in this chapter pertain to commonly held beliefs related to the prison in general and the private prison more specifically. Let us now consider a few of these beliefs and see what judicial and print medium portrayals reveal. This consideration will permit conclusions to be made about the advantages and disadvantages of privatization and its potential for supporting prison specialization initiatives.

The first belief that persists about the contemporary prison is that a profit motive leads to civil rights violations. Opponents of privatization argue that when profit is introduced into the prison, it quickly becomes the dominant operational objective. This belief suggests that the pursuit of profit results in the degradation of the prison environment, which, it is reasoned, culminates in a situation where the inmate is perceived as little more than a "means to an end." Inmates are reduced to the status of "commodities" and are viewed as little more than objects without civil rights. Moreover, opponents surmise that private operators will reduce both staff and training levels to increase profit margins, further placing inmates at risk of mistreatment. While it is easy hypothetically to link profit to mistreatment, as some journalists did, little evidence was found to suggest that lawsuits filed against either sector are the direct result of efficient or profitable operations. More specifically, of those operational areas that emerged from judicial records that can practically be linked to a financial incentive, one half suggested no relationship between profit and civil rights violations. For example, four areas of prison operations appear to be especially good candidates for financial manipulation. These areas are living conditions, physical conditions, medical treatment, and physical security. A consideration of the frequency with which lawsuits were filed alleging violations in these four areas reveals that the private sector experienced a greater frequency (in comparison with the public sector) of allegations pertaining to living and physical conditions, but fewer allegations related to medical treatment and physical security. Based solely upon the frequency of these allegations, it is difficult to determine the effect (if any) of profit on inmate treatment. Until evidence is found to suggest otherwise, this belief must be considered baseless as it is not supported by statements appearing in prisoner complaints or in judicial statements made in response to those complaints. Neither of the sectors deserves vilification for attempting to operate efficiently or for profit, until definitive evidence is found to suggest that such a motive is antithetical to the promotion of the public welfare or detrimental to the inmate population. Similarly, this finding further suggests that private operators are as capable of adhering to constitutional mandates as are public operators. While the operational ideologies of the sectors differ, no conclusive evidence was found to suggest that the private sector is more prone to constitutional violations than is the public sector. In fact, one might argue that the private sector's young age should have naturally produced an even greater number of allegations across all violation categories, since it has had less time (in comparison with the public sector) to mature or implement appropriate policy and procedure. Since no evidence was found to suggest otherwise, one must assume that private operations are no more problematic than are traditional approaches. And finally, since private operators appear to be as capable of adhering to constitutional mandates as are public operators, there is little to prevent the private sector from assuming a position of prominence under prison specialization initiatives.

There is also a pervasive belief among many penologists that the judiciary, to some degree, still honors its traditional "hands-off approach" when asked to intervene in prison affairs. A **hands-off approach** refers to the judiciary's hesitancy to intervene in prison operations. While such an approach was common in the past, it does not accurately describe the judiciary's current sentiment. No evidence was uncovered to suggest hesitancy by the judiciary when addressing the actions of prison operators. In fact, just the opposite appeared true, because the judiciary seemed to speak its mind freely. While these judicial statements were at times quite stern, they were also overwhelmingly corrective and nurturing in nature—especially when dealing with the private sector. For example, in *Bowman v. CCA* (2000), the presiding judge reminded one particular operator that the American Medical Association's Council on Ethics and Judicial Affairs has established standards that must be met by physicians awarded "bonuses" based upon reductions in medical expenditures. Not only did the court remind the defendants of these standards, but it also provided them with excerpts.

Similarly, in one of the most sensational cases reviewed (*Kesler v. Brazoria County*, 1998), the court stated that

> overseeing and working within a jail or prison environment is a difficult task. Jails and prisons are by their very nature involuntary destinations for persons who have a demonstrated proclivity for anti-social, and often violent, conduct. Nevertheless, jail and prison officials bear the difficult burden of balancing the requirements imposed by the nature of their charges against rights those prisoners do not forfeit simply because they have been adjudicated guilty of some crime. Administrators must ensure the safety of their staffs, visitors, the public, and the inmates themselves.

This statement clearly shows that the judiciary recognizes the inherent difficulty prison operators face when caring for those who are incarcerated. Statements of this kind remind officials that they must take their duties seriously and that a criminal conviction does not result in the absolute forfeiture of one's civil rights. The court suggested indirectly that prison operations involve a "sacred trust" integral to a democratic government that is built on the concept of justice.

In *McKnight v. Rees* (1996), the Court further reminded prison officials that

> [t]he public undoubtedly has an interest in maintaining secure and efficient correctional facilities. We need not recite the litany of public benefits traditionally associated with maintaining an effective penal system here. Suffice it to say that it is beyond peradventure that correctional officers working for a private, for-profit corporation that has contracted with the state are serving a public interest by operating Tennessee's prison facilities.

Again, the court reminded all parties connected with this suit of the public trust involved in prison operations. To ensure this trust is protected, the court went on to propound the merits of implementing a comprehensive monitoring program. This approach would require the contracting governmental jurisdiction to oversee private sector operations to ensure that all parties involved are adequately fulfilling their legal responsibility. The court encouraged such an approach as a way to protect everyone involved. Of course, the implementation of a monitoring program was a suggestion intended to correct operational inadequacies. Various judicial statements, when considered collectively, suggest that the judiciary recognizes a value in prison privatization. This is a significant finding, since it is the judiciary that is best positioned to sound a warning should privatization provide little or no social benefit. By nurturing the private sector, by reminding the private sector of its responsibility to both the inmate and taxpayer, and by failing to oppose its involvement in prison operations, the judiciary has clearly given privatization its endorsement.

Finally, it is generally believed that a desire for profit and financial savings is the driving force behind prison privatization. This being the case, one would expect to find financial topics being reflected in a majority of the print medium's articles; this belief is largely unsubstantiated. Though financial issues were mentioned in a great number of articles, they appeared less frequently than did the issue of institutional crowding. This finding suggests that while the public is interested in financial issues, it is even more interested in acquiring enough prison space to ensure prisoner safety. Thus, support for prison privatization as a way to promote efficiency and acquire additional space will probably extend well into the future. Furthermore, if the print medium's coverage is any indication of the public's interests in these topics, the public will probably embrace specialization as a mechanism to further promote operational efficiency and community safety.

Summary

Overall, a consideration of judicial and print medium portrayals yields a substantial amount of information about how judges and journalists perceive privatization. Reviews of judicial documents failed to uncover a consensus among federal judges to suggest that privatization is problematic or that private operations jeopardize the civil rights of inmate populations. In fact, in only a few cases did judicial statements appear unfavorable. Since the judiciary did not associate a profit rationale with inmate mistreatment, there is little reason to oppose the private sector's involvement in prison operations or to deny it a place of prominence under specialization initiatives.

Furthermore, while the print medium focuses a substantial amount of attention on financial issues, the topic of prison crowding garners even more attention. Journalists clearly recognize that prison overcrowding has forced officials to leave dangerous offenders in the community rather than place them inside the prison. To a lesser degree they also realize that crowding accelerates the pace at which inmates are paroled and discharged. Since prison privatization promises to lower operating costs and provide the additional space needed, it will undoubtedly continue to attract support well into the future. By acquiring the much-needed additional space we will have the assurance that the prison will remain an institution that has the capacity to house society's most dangerous offenders. Additional space will also help guarantee that parole and discharge dates remain undisturbed. The observations detailed in this chapter, when taken in their entirety, suggest a strong public interest in reducing correctional expenditure while ensuring that our prison system is able to incarcerate those offenders who pose the greatest risk to society. Interests of this kind may drive current political leadership increasingly to capitalize on the strengths of both sectors—the publicly operated prison to house the dangerous and high-risk inmate and the privately operated prison to house the less dangerous and lower-risk inmate. Public safety interests and operational efficiency will continue to contribute to the popularity of prison privatization and will stimulate a growing interest in the specialization of the contemporary prison.

Chapter Highlights

1. Information obtained from our nation's judges and print journalists provides insight into prison operations not available elsewhere.
2. Prison privatization refers to the contractual process whereby the government pays a private corporation for the construction and/or operation of correctional facilities.
3. Many early prisons were privately operated.
4. The government's pursuit, apprehension, prosecution, and punishment of the offender are relatively recent developments. For most of human history, these pursuits were private affairs.
5. The reemergence of prison privatization can be traced to the 1960s, when social dissent increased throughout the United States.

6. The Vietnam War polarized America's citizenry and caused many to question the government's role in modern society.

7. Social dissatisfaction with the government has led to criticism of its monopolization of correctional services.

8. In the mid-1980s, local jurisdictions in Tennessee and Florida began to experiment with the privatization of jail facilities.

9. Kentucky was the first state to partially privatize its prison system.

10. Privatization has become a popular method for acquiring additional prison space.

11. A typical private sector inmate is one who has been convicted of a relatively minor offense.

12. The public sector retains offenders believed to be especially dangerous and who pose a significant risk of escape.

13. The average sentence served by inmates in public prisons is more than twice that served by private sector inmates.

14. The judiciary is unconvinced that a relationship exists between profit and inmate mistreatment.

15. The issues of overcrowding and operational efficiency dominate the media's coverage of prison privatization.

16. Coverage of prison privatization by our nation's print medium has become more neutral since 1986, the approximate year of the topic's reemergence.

17. Prison privatization and prison specialization are complementary pursuits.

Discussion Questions

1. What social factors have helped promote the privatization of government services?

2. Of those advantages associated with privatization, which have the most merit? Which have the least?

3. Are there disadvantages associated with privatization? If so, what are they?

4. What does a review of lawsuits reveal about the way the judiciary perceives prison privatization?

5. What does a review of newspaper articles reveal about the way the print medium perceives prison privatization?

6. Are there parallels between the way judges and journalists perceive privatization? If so, what are they?

7. In addition to judges and journalists, are there any other professional groups that could provide insight into privatization? If so, how might

their insights contribute to our understanding of the private prison sector?

8. What type of inmate does the private sector tend to house? How do these inmates differ from those housed in public prisons?

9. What role might the private sector play under prison specialization initiatives?

10. Do the findings presented within this chapter suggest a climate favorable for prison specialization? Explain.

Sources

Blakely, C. 2005. *America's Prisons: The Movement toward Profit and Privatization*. Florida: Brown Walker Press.

Cases cited

Bowman v. Correction Corporation of America (CCA) et al., U.S. District Court for the Middle District of Tennessee, Nashville Division (No. 3:96–1142); Entered March 15, 2000.

Bridgeforth v. Ramsey et al., U.S. Court of Appeals for the Tenth Circuit (No. 99–6179); Filed November 2, 1999.

Citrano and Chapman v. Allen Correctional Center (CV 94–1076); Filed June 14, 1995.

Kesler et al. v. Brazoria County Sheriff King et al., U.S. District Court for the Southern District of Texas, Galveston Division (No. G-96–703); Entered December 7, 1998.

McKnight v. Rees et al., U.S. Court of Appeals for the Sixth Circuit (No. 95–5398); Filed July 10, 1996.

Perry v. Rose et al., U.S. Court of Appeals for the Sixth Circuit (No. 995–240); Filed February 7, 2000.

Scott v. District of Columbia et al., U.S. District Court for the District of Columbia (98–01645(HHK)); Filed November 22, 1999.

West v. Keating, U.S. Court of Appeals for the Tenth Circuit (No. 00–7129); Filed August 13, 2001.

Newspapers Cited

Advocate. May 21, 2000. Private Prisons, State Obligation. Baton Rouge, LA. p. 10-B.

Albuquerque Journal. August 31, 1999. Prison Violence Trends Examined. Loie Fedteau, p. C-1.

Austin American Statesman. December 17, 1989. The Promise of Private Prisons//Kyle Facility Shoots for Quality. Henry Krausse, p. B1.

Houston Chronicle. February 20, 1987. Bill Would Allow Contracts for Private Prisons. Mark Toohey, p. 14.

Milwaukee Journal Sentinel. October 3, 1998. State to Probe Alleged Abuse of Inmates in Tennessee Complaints Made at Prison. Richard Jones, p. 1.

Milwaukee Journal Sentinel. August 12, 1999. State Inmates in Private Prison File Suit, Federal Lawsuits Allege Guards Tortured, Violated Civil Rights of Wisconsin Prisoners in Tennessee. Richard Jones, p. 1.

Omaha World Herald. August 6, 1986. Company Hopes to Build and Run 1st Private Prison. p. 1.

Palm Beach Post. February 9, 1997. Private Prisons Scoff at Fla. Law. Charles Elmore, p. 1A.

The Patriot-News. April 9, 1987. Panel Says State Should Continue to Prohibit Privately Run Prisons. Kenn Marshall, p. B6.

Plain Dealer. May 25, 1995. Town Profits from Prison. Joe Hallinan, p. 5A.

Tulsa World. October 18, 1998. CCA Critics Point to Problems at Facilities. Tim Hoover, p. 1.

Virginian-Pilot. November 8, 1995. Currituck Takes Steps to Lure Private Prison to the County. Anne Saita, p. B2.

Washington Post. October 10, 1988. D.C. Looks at Prisons Run for Profit: Private Facilities May Ease Crowding. Saundra Torry, p. A1.

Washington Post. June 13, 1999. Private Prisons: The Bottom Line. Ted Strickland, p. B1.

If prison officials continue to ignore offender reform, society will ultimately demand the reform of the prison itself.

Chapter Five

Where Do We Go from Here?

I have stated several times throughout this book that if the prison is to promote community safety effectively, it must first change the manner in which it views and approaches the inmate. Any attempt to improve the prison is a grand undertaking indeed, because penologists have long struggled with this very same pursuit. Regardless of the many attempts and subsequent failures that have occurred in this quest, improvement cannot occur until it is first suggested, as it is in this chapter. Complicating this endeavor is the inherent difficulty in determining the extent of change needed as well as identifying those changes that are both socially and financially acceptable. The anticipated social benefit of any particular change must always be weighed against its ultimate cost. While there are a myriad ways to improve the contemporary prison, specialization provides an opportunity to make the prison more efficient and effective in its ability to promote community safety. By proposing such a progressive change, I hope that other penologists will similarly offer proposals that might produce the same result. If this occurs, this book will have begun a process that is beneficial to all.

Generally speaking, improvement occurs only after it has been sug-gested, and a suggestion is always the result of a question. The question that has guided this book has been "How can we make the prison more effective in its ability to promote public safety?" It is this very question that first gave rise to the concept of the specialized prison. Similarly, this chapter also begins with a question—"Where do we go from here?" This rather simple question implies that

- options do exist concerning the paths down which the prison may travel, demonstrating that its future has not been predetermined;
- while the prison is not doomed to any one particular fate, setting the prison on a new path requires open debate, discussion, and determination; and
- while there is uncertainty about which particular path is the most beneficial, we must always ensure that change will bring about the greatest good for the greatest number of people in the shortest possible time.

By now you will have noticed that this book is based upon a belief that society is no longer willing to support prisons that provide little return on its investment. Citizens increasingly contend that they deserve more from their correctional professionals and their institutions. Criticisms of this nature are often based on the observation that a large percentage of the ex-inmate population is reinstitutionalized at some point following release. I have personally known inmates who have served as many as seven separate prison sentences. I am confident that all prison officials will tell you that they see the same offenders repeat-edly returning to prison. The observation of critics that many inmates have served multiple prison terms is certainly valid. These critics argue that the prison should not have revolving doors through which the same offender returns again and again and again. It is because of this dilemma that progressive penologists and practitioners recognize the need for prison reform. However, the extent of change that is appropri-ate is open to debate. While some believe that the effectiveness of the prison can be greatly enhanced with a few modifications, others, like me, believe that substantial change is warranted. For the most part, as the pendulum of prison reform has swung in one direction, it has inevitably swung back toward the other. When looking at the prison's history, one will not see a smooth evolution, but a series of changes and change-reversals that has made it difficult for it to evolve in any meaningful fashion. Yes, the prison has changed dramatically since its inception, especially in the area of inmate treatment, but how different today's prisons would have been if only innovative thinkers had been allowed to guide the prison down a more socially responsible path!

> *What if . . . the prison had evolved in a smooth and purpose-driven fashion? Would it differ significantly from the contemporary prison?*

One obstacle to the prison's ability to operate more effectively is the confusion that continues to exist about its overall purpose. Of course, a thorough consideration of the prison's traditional objectives becomes essential when proposing operational changes. Many correctional practitioners erroneously believe that the prison's sole objective is containment. Yet such an approach is not supported by the prison's own history or its traditional objectives. Furthermore, containment by itself has always proven ineffective in promoting public safety. In fact, there appears to be little, if any, appreciable effect of even the longest of prison terms on crime rates. If harsh punishments such as incarceration and three-strikes laws actually produced a deterrent effect, recidivism rates among ex-inmates would be much lower than they are currently. This is precisely why the designers of the early prison pursued inmate reform. To more effectively promote community safety, incarceration must (when appropriate) be coupled with a reform ideology. This is not to suggest that all inmates are good candidates for reform, because they are not. But it does suggest that inmate reform must be a recognized and valued pursuit.

Measures of Effectiveness

When suggesting institutional reform, we must have a thorough understanding of the prison's current level of performance. Performance measures not only reveal the effectiveness or ineffectiveness of the prison, but also make it possible for us to determine the effects resulting from reform initiatives. In essence, a baseline measurement must always be established to permit pre- and postchange comparisons. However, there is disagreement over which areas of a prison's operations are most appropriate for assessment and reform. The source of this controversy can be traced to the ideologies of normalization and less eligibility. Of course, whereas adherents of normalization prefer recidivism as a performance measure, advocates of less eligibility prefer measures such as institutional capacity and fiscal efficiency. While advocates of normalization believe that the prison's primary objective is the promotion of the public's long-term safety, supporters of less eligibility value operations that can house large numbers of inmates as cheaply as possible. As an advocate of increased public safety via inmate reform, I am frequently reminded by practitioners that inmate reform is but one way to promote public safety. They claim that public safety can be advanced through the prison's ability to securely incapacitate the offender and that containment is an acceptable penal pursuit. Such an observation is indeed correct up to a certain point. Incapacitation does promote public safety, but to what extent it does so is difficult to determine. One must recognize that there is a significant difference between these two diametrically opposed views—one promotes the public's long-term well-being and the other promotes short-term security. I would suggest that any approach that blithely ignores its own long-term effects should be avoided. So what characteristic should be measured? This determination is paramount, since it will affect both the inmate population and society for many years to come. As we consider this question in greater depth, remember that advocates of less eligibility prefer to use internal performance measures as an assessment tool. **Internal performance measures** consider prison characteristics that are largely obscured from the public's view. Common internal measures include

- capacity level (considered a measure of a prison's ability to protect society from predation),
- reductions in annual expenditure (considered a measure of a prison administration's fiscal responsibility and conservatism),
- the number of months a prison has been escape-free (considered a measure of a prison's ability to operate securely),

- the number of days/months that a prison has operated without inmate or staff injury (considered a measure of a prison's ability to operate safely), and
- the number of institutional misconduct reports processed each year (considered a measure of a prison administration's ability to sanction and control inmate behavior).

While internal measures of performance do have a place in the assessment process, they are not especially informative or meaningful to the average citizen. In fact, they reveal little about the prison's social value, since they fail to measure performance against well-established and easily understood objectives. Instead, internal measures are subjective in nature, as their overall value is largely determined by how they are interpreted by the prison's own officials. Therefore they are open to manipulation or misconstruction—to the advantage of the prison itself. Similarly, this approach also creates a natural incentive for officials to measure only those characteristics that positively reflect on their performance, ignoring others that would reflect less favorably. Thus, internal measures potentially give the public a distorted portrayal of the prison's true value and contribution to their safety. Proponents of this approach appear to view the prison as being fundamentally different from other institutions. Such a belief permits them to ignore the expectations and objectives that have long been associated with prison operations. In doing so, they fail to recognize the relationship that has historically existed between social institutions and the individual citizen and between the prison and the inmate (more on this later in the chapter). As a result of using internal measures of performance,

- the institution itself becomes the focus of a prison administration's attention (primarily its capacity level as well as its budgetary requirements), while the individual inmate is ignored,
- prison officials are allowed to determine what constitutes "success" and when success has been achieved,
- prison officials are able to conceal operational inadequacies by directing attention toward those areas that clearly suggest success while ignoring others that reflect poorly on their performance, and
- public safety becomes a distant consideration.

As you see, internal measurements of a prison's performance can be manipulated rather easily. These measures tend to be self-serving and fail to reflect a genuine interest in the public's well-being. Opponents of internal performance measures assert that external measures more accurately reflect a prison's social contribution. **External performance measures** consider characteristics that provide insight into the prison's ability to promote the public's long-term interest. Advocates of external measures recognize that the public's well-being is greatly affected by every offender whom the prison returns to society. They also believe that the individual inmate must always be the focus of the prison's attention. Proponents of this approach recognize that the purpose of most social institutions is to address issues at the individual level, for it is at this level that problems can most easily be identified and addressed. For example, the hospital seeks to maintain and improve the health of a community, but it does this by focusing on the individual citizen. To measure the effectiveness or social value of the hospital, we simply measure the number of diseases or conditions that it detects, treats, and cures. In doing so, we are using an external measure of performance that is easily understood and accepted by the average citizen. Similarly, public schools seek to produce a competitive and wealthy nation, but they do this by focusing on the individual student. To measure the effectiveness of the school one must simply consider scores obtained on standardized exams or even graduation rates, both of which are external performance measures that provide the average citizen with an easily understood and widely accepted gauge of the school's effectiveness. If you are especially perceptive, you will have realized that in each of these examples, it is both the individual and society—in that order—that benefit from the actions of the institution. Generally speaking, institutions are powerless to implement broad and sweeping social change, but are able effectively to address issues at the individual level. The prison as an institution is quite similar to the hospital and the school. The only difference among these three institutions is that the prison miserably fails to promote society's long-term interest by ignoring the individual, which results in its inability to promote public safety.

What if . . . external performance measures were used to assess the prison? Would its officials protest?

Much like the hospital and school, the prison's effectiveness is best measured through a consideration of external measures. The most appropriate external measure of performance is its recidivism rate, which reflects the prison's ability to detect, treat, and cure antisocial and maladaptive behaviors. Remember that recidivism rates indicate the percentage of the ex-inmate population that is subsequently convicted of a new crime. Recidivism rates can be measured in a multitude of ways, most of which differ only in the time frame under consideration. For example, some penologists suggest that recidivism should be measured over the 6-, 12-, or 18-month period directly following an inmate's release. Unfortunately, this approach limits our ability to determine the long-term effects of imprisonment. The most easily understood approach, and I would argue the most appropriate measure of recidivism, considers the percentage of ex-inmates who are convicted of a new crime at any time following release. Such an open-ended measure permits an undistorted view of the prison's ability to improve public safety over long periods of time. This approach is more informative for both the practitioner and the average citizen. Furthermore, an open-ended measure of recidivism would help control for the short-term effect of parole, thereby further isolating the effects of incarceration. Recidivism is an especially useful and informative measure since it

- requires prison officials to recognize inmate reform as a valuable objective,
- quantifies prison performance in an easily understood and universally accepted measure, and
- ensures that prison officials (be they public or private) are accountable to the citizenry, reestablishing community safety as an operational objective.

As this last point indicates, recidivism rates are an especially appropriate assessment tool regardless of whether a prison is publicly or privately operated or whether it is a custodial, professional, or specialized institution. Thus, as a performance measure, recidivism is equally insightful regardless of the operational objective being sought. The question then is "How do we lower recidivism rates?"

The Answer May Be Prison Specialization

One of the most significant assertions made in this book is that there are just two groups of inmates: those who are changeable and others who are not. The acceptance of this assertion is the first step toward lowering recidivism rates and making society a safer place. If we accept this assertion as an unmitigated fact, we must acknowledge that a portion of the inmate population should be actively targeted for treatment. By relentlessly targeting only those inmates most likely to benefit from treatment, the prison becomes more fiscally responsible and increases the chances of helping produce lasting inmate reform, which, in turn, would lead to reduced crime rates. The problem of course is how to determine which inmates are changeable and which are not. One way to determine into which group any particular inmate falls is through a consideration of his/her demeanor. To the contemporary practitioner a consideration of an inmate's demeanor with treatment in view remains an alien concept. Under specialization initiatives, a consideration of an inmate's demeanor would help prison officials determine

- which inmates are reform-oriented and which would resist treatment,
- the form of intervention(s) most appropriate for each particular inmate, and
- the "type" of prison best suited to house a particular inmate.

A consideration of an inmate's demeanor and the proper use of this information form the basis of prison specialization. Since this means recognizing that there are changeable inmates, prison officials operating under this initiative would be forced to admit that

- treatment is an appropriate course of action for some portion of the inmate population and not a realistic pursuit for others,
- changeable and unchangeable inmates must be separated to eliminate the corrupting effect of the intractable inmate,
- the inmate population is not a homogeneous group,
- each individual inmate is unique, and so too are the personal challenges each faces,

- treatment must be customized to meet the needs of each inmate,
- by treating only changeable inmates, a better use of scarce correctional resources is achieved, and
- in addition to containment, inmate reform is a valuable correctional objective.

An acknowledgment that changeable (tractable) inmates really do exist challenges the popular belief among officials that all inmates are unchangeable (intractable). Such an acknowledgment strikes at the very heart of contemporary penal practice. Generally speaking, every offender currently sent to prison is believed to be similar to every other offender. In this respect, all inmates are assumed to be intractable; most of them are denied the opportunity to undergo intensive treatment and to participate in treatment free from the influence of those who would impede their reform. Let there be no doubt about it, tractable inmates do exist. The exact percentage of the inmate population that is tractable may be difficult to estimate, but based upon personal observation as well as insight given to me by others, their numbers might be much larger than many assume. If I am correct, the prison not only makes it difficult for tractable inmates to achieve a reformed state, but directly contributes to the crime problem by not providing quality treatment programs, thereby failing in its responsibility to protect current program participants from the corrupting influence of the intractable inmate.

> *What if . . . intractable and tractable inmates were housed separately? Would recidivism rates decrease?*

Recognition of the existence of changeable and unchangeable inmates prompts the recognition of the need for specifically designed prisons to deal with each of these groups. Generalized institutional placement must be seen as a practice that perpetuates crime and disorder. While I have previously presented material on the custodial prison, the real challenge that awaits penologists is in creating the professional prison. Yes, there is a place for the custodial institution under prison specialization initiatives, but there is also a recognized need for the professional prison. While a certain percentage of the inmate population will always warrant strict physical control, a certain percentage will benefit from a wide range of quality treatment programs. An emphasis on treatment and responsibility would help tractable inmates better adjust to the prison environment, and a normalized approach to prison operations is a definite precursor to their subsequent successful social assimilation.

Knowing that prison specialization requires the creation of the professional prison, we should also note that our current prison system is rapidly becoming a hybrid system. A **hybrid system** comprises both publicly and privately operated prisons. The system recognizes that each sector has its own unique way of dealing with the inmate population; in essence, each has its own operational advantages. While recognizing the differences between the sectors, we must also celebrate them. Many of these differences are directly attributable to the type of inmate the sector houses. Of course the public sector is made up of older institutions ideally suited for inmate control and the prevention of escape. These prisons are well suited for holding the serious and dangerous offender. Conversely, private prisons house the less serious and less hardened offender for relatively short periods of time. The environment of the private prison is much more open and conducive to a treatment ideology. It stands to reason that since the private prison houses the less serious inmate, it should assume the role of the "professional prison." Remember that the professional prison

- normalizes the prison environment,
- emphasizes treatment,
- emphasizes inmate accountability,
- recognizes that inmates have in many cases never been taught the value of responsible behavior, and
- provides opportunities for inmates to hone their decision-making skills.

Let me reemphasize this point. The private sector is ideally positioned to assume the role of the professional prison. There is simply nothing about the private sector that disqualifies it from serving in this capacity. In fact, the literature is replete with studies that suggest the private sector is well suited for this assignment. For example, a study completed in the latter part of the 1990s found that the private sector offered its inmates a greater range of education and treatment programming than did the public sector. Researchers also found that the private sector either equaled or outperformed the public sector with regard to the percentage of inmates it screened and released to community treatment programs. Furthermore, the private sector had a greater percentage of its inmate population complete literacy and vocational training courses (Archambeault and Deis, 1996). A more recent study found similar results, prompting the authors to challenge the popular belief that the expense of treatment initiatives would dissuade the private sector from offering rehabilitative programming (Armstrong and Mackenzie, 2003). Another study asked prison administrators (both public and private) to provide their perceptions on a host of issues pertaining to private sector operations. These practitioners indicated that in their collective opinion, there is no basis to support the common assumption that the private sector will curtail treatment to maximize profit (Bumphus, Blakely, and DeMichele, 2001). Finally, it should be noted that the private sector has twice the number of inmates participating in drug treatment programs that the public sector has (data provided by the Criminal Justice Institute). This finding suggests that the private sector is addressing an important contributory factor long associated with improper and maladaptive behavior—the use of illegal intoxicants. Most research on the use of intoxicants and their link to criminality finds that more than one half of all inmates had an illegal substance in their system at the time they committed the offense that resulted in their current term of confinement. Data supplied by the Criminal Justice Institute further reveal that the private sector has a greater percentage of psychiatrists, caseworkers, and counselors working in its prisons than has the public sector. These studies collectively reinforce my position that the private sector is both willing and able to provide treatment.

Now that you have read this book, you have probably asked yourself (I hope more than once) whether prison specialization is feasible. My answer to that question is a resounding "yes"! Prison specialization *is* feasible and the private sector can play a vital role in this initiative. The sooner this process begins, the less effort it will take to implement these suggestions. The time to implement these suggestions is now. If society is serious about lowering crime rates, then sweeping prison reform is an absolute must. Of course, if we continue to do what we have always done, then we will always get what we have always got, that is, unnecessarily high recidivism rates. But how do we begin? To introduce specialization into our contemporary prison system as quickly and as effortlessly as possible, I suggest that it be implemented in six distinct phases. Here is my proposal.

Phase 1: Open Debate and Discussion

This phase would involve open debate and discussion about the merits and challenges of prison specialization. Of particular value would be the viewpoints of our most progressive penologists and practitioners, who, drawing upon their vast experience of and familiarity with the prison system, would provide a great deal of insight into the advantages, disadvantages, and feasibility of prison specialization. Interaction of this nature could occur through roundtable discussions and paper presentations at national conferences of the American Correctional Association (an organization made up mainly of correctional professionals), the **Academy of Criminal Justice Sciences,** and the **American Society of Criminology** (these latter two organizations are made up mainly of academicians, criminal justice researchers, and students). Other professional organizations at both the national and regional levels could prove equally useful in this process. Feedback from conference attendees would be especially helpful in identifying and solving complex problems relating to classification and policy issues. Professional forums of this nature are specifically designed to promote interaction, discourse, and exploration. In fact, the conferences held by these organizations routinely serve as the initial proving grounds for ideas pertaining to all three components of the criminal justice system (police, judiciary, and corrections). These organizations also publish journals that are well suited for taking innovative ideas to a much larger audience that is thus provided an opportunity to weigh in on subjects of interest. This phase would help spark a healthy national debate about the nature of contemporary corrections and the direction the future prison needs to take. Debate, discussion, and scholarship form the basis for this phase.

Phase 2: Initial Test Site Application

In this phase, proponents of specialization would put into practice what was learned in the previous phase, assuming that some degree of consensus exists about the merits of this approach. In essence, we would proceed if and only if there is support for specialization. At this stage, researchers would pay particular attention to specialization's ability to reduce correctional expenditures while lowering recidivism rates. A pilot program would be undertaken to permit a short-term (36–60-month) study. Administrative, treatment, and security staff of willing jurisdictions would be briefed on the philosophy and operational objectives of the initiative. Prespecialization measurements related to a wide range of institutional characteristics would be gathered and analyzed. These would provide the basis for a pre- and postapplication comparison. While it would prove useful to have as many facilities involved as possible, even a few would yield enough data for the purposes of initial assessment. These initial sites could, if it were determined beneficial, operate continuously until the conclusion of the sixth and final phase. For every site selected, a control site would be chosen to further isolate specialization's effects. It would also prove beneficial to pay particular attention to those inmates who are granted parole versus those who are discharged. This would further isolate any benefits associated with specialization by controlling for the effects of community supervision. Test site application forms the basis for this phase.

Phase 3: Open Debate and Discussion Revisited

Once the initial test site phase is completed, we would return to a process in which our leading penologists and practitioners discussed the advantages and disadvantages of specialization. Test site data would be used to determine the ability of the specialized prison to promote operational efficiency and lower recidivism rates. The data gathered during pre- and postapplication periods would be compared. If it appears that this approach holds promise, additional test sites would be selected for participation. Discussion, debate, and scholarship based upon test site data form the basis for this phase.

Phase 4: Follow-Up Test Site Application

In this phase, we would again put into practice what we learned in the previous phases, paying particular attention to any areas of interest that warrant additional attention. Modifications to the initial test site design could be implemented to address operational concerns. Depending on initial test site findings, this phase may be rather short in duration (12–36 months) or, if necessary, substantially longer (36–120 months). Again, it would prove beneficial to have as many jurisdictions and operators involved as feasible. When possible, all previous test sites would continue operation, thereby providing an ongoing point of comparison. This would help isolate the effects of those modifications that may have been previously implemented. This phase allows for the collection of data that span a substantial time period. Admittedly, even a study that spans a full ten-year period would provide only a limited degree of insight into the long-term effects of specialization. Nevertheless, this insight would prove invaluable when assessing the strengths of the specialized prison. The collection and comparison of data from initial, follow-up, and control facilities forms the basis for this phase.

Phase 5: Open Debate and Discussion Re-Revisited

Once the follow-up test site application has been completed, after paying particular attention to operating costs, classification processes, program completion rates, and recidivism levels, we would again return to open discussion about the advantages and disadvantages of specialization. Theory, specific operational challenges, and research findings would fuel this part of the process. In this phase, the data gathered from all the sites would be thoroughly analyzed and compared. Comparisons would be made between

- pre- and postapplication sites in phase 2,
- pre- and postapplication sites in phase 4,
- all phase 2 and phase 4 test and control sites (on both pre- and postapplication data), and
- inmates who were paroled and discharged.

Discussion, debate, and scholarship provide the basis for this phase.

Phase 6: Adoption/Abandonment

During this phase one of two actions would be taken. First, assuming that the testing process went well, prison systems nationwide would be encouraged to pursue specialization. This would involve a great deal of education to familiarize decision makers and the citizenry with the advantages of this approach. This could be completed relatively quickly, perhaps in a five- to ten-year period.

Conversely, if it were determined that specialization provides fewer advantages than first expected, it might be partially abandoned or modified. **Partial abandonment** or **modification** signifies the adoption of those parts of specialization that prove to be advantageous while dropping or modifying those that are less so. It is important to note that what one jurisdiction finds beneficial, another jurisdiction may not consider advantageous. Therefore, partial abandonment or modification may be necessary to meet the unique needs and challenges faced by the U.S. prison systems. For example, while a particular prison system may subscribe to the tenets of specialization, its officials may prefer to house tractable and intractable inmates in separate areas of the same facility. This would ensure that each group is being dealt with appropriately while eliminating the corrupting influence of the intractable inmate. This prison system is still adhering to the fundamental principles of specialization, but in a modified form. **Complete abandonment,** on the other hand, is a rejection of prison specialization in its entirety. Of course, this would be the result if researchers discovered that specialization provides little or no operational advantage over our current approach. It is important to understand that complete abandonment should never be interpreted as a theoretical or operational failure. Why? Well, to understand my reasoning, you must first realize that all initiatives have both primary and secondary objectives. A **primary objective** is the dominant goal of a particular activity, and a **secondary objective** is subordinate to the primary goal but is nonetheless important. Even when an initiative has been unable to achieve its primary objective, it has, in all probability, achieved a number of its secondary objectives, which can have significant benefits for society. Before addressing the primary and secondary objectives of specialization initiatives, and to further clarify this point, let us consider a popular criminal justice program, **DARE**

(Drug Abuse Resistance Education). This has long been a favorite program among our nation's fifth and sixth grade students and is also popular among school districts, with about 70 percent having an active DARE curriculum. DARE uses police officers, animated robots, and costumed characters to teach children about the perils of drug use. DARE also provides its young participants with useful tools to help them resist negative peer pressure. Introduced in 1983 in Los Angeles, DARE has as its primary objective the elimination of drug use among its graduates. While this is certainly a worthwhile goal, researchers have consistently found evidence suggesting that DARE has no appreciable effect upon the actions of its graduates. In essence, they claim that DARE fails to achieve its primary objective. Citing this failure, opponents of DARE suggest that the resources devoted to its continuation should instead be redirected to the development of a more effective program, which, no doubt, is commendable. However, many individuals, like me, are not prepared to abandon DARE, because even though it may be unable to achieve its primary objective, it overwhelmingly succeeds in accomplishing its secondary objectives, which include establishing a positive relationship between the youth and police, humanizing law enforcement officials, and providing youth with a contact person within the local police department. It does all this while sending a positive message to the community about the value of children. In a similar sense, even if specialization were to be proven ineffective at lowering recidivism rates, a number of secondary objectives would have been achieved. This would prove that the time and effort devoted to its consideration had not been wasted. The secondary objectives of specialization include

- increased understanding of the contemporary penal system,
- increased debate about current penal practices,
- identification of better classification processes,
- increased familiarization with correctional objectives,
- identification of additional ways to promote prison efficiency,
- increased insight into how inmate reform might be achieved, and
- the commencement of a national debate about the future direction of the prison.

So even if specialization were to be completely rejected, its consideration would have helped facilitate debate, discussion, and exploration. Of course increased dialogue and a willingness to consider new ideas are both necessary for the reinvigoration of penology and the advancement of penal thought.

> *What if . . . penology was again to become a dynamic field? Would innovative and progressive ideas challenge contemporary penal practice? Explain.*

Areas of Concern

As this phased approach to the study of specialization progresses, there are four specific areas of concern that require further consideration. These areas recognize the follwing needs.

- Penologists and prison officials must devise and implement methods to eliminate arbitrary decision-making practices pertaining to classification processes. To ensure that specialization initiatives are implemented correctly and that the best candidates for treatment are identified and included in the treatment process, classification must be undertaken in a fair and impartial fashion. Inmates and citizens alike should be assured that all decisions are based on sound information and not on the personal likes or dislikes of those in authority. In essence, measures must be implemented to ensure that the label "intractable" is never assigned improperly or used as a punitive measure. One way to address this concern is to ensure diversity among decision makers with regard to race, religion, and political affiliation. Provisions should also be made to record and justify all classification decisions, establish decision-making guidelines, provide for supervisory review, and permit inmates an opportunity to appeal classification decisions. Through ensuring diversity among decision makers and making the process transparent, concerns of this nature can be greatly reduced while the integrity of the process is increased.
- Penologists and prison officials must devise a method to assess an inmate's desire and suitability for treatment accurately. Such a determination would require the development of appropriate

questionnaires, formalized interview and observational processes, and, when necessary, in-depth investigations. Complicating this already difficult undertaking is the inevitability that one part of this process will occasionally contradict another. For example, what is the proper course of action when an inmate claims a desire for treatment but staff observations indicate otherwise? Furthermore, what is the proper course of action if an inmate claims a desire for treatment but family and friends indicate otherwise? We must determine how much weight to assign to an inmate's spoken word versus how much weight should be given to staff observations and investigations. This concern specifically requires that safeguards be implemented to ensure that inmates do not manipulate the system and that inmates are not classified incorrectly, both of which would compromise the integrity of classification processes.

- Penologists and prison officials must develop methods for making adjustments to the classification process based upon changes in an inmate's demeanor. For example, tractable inmates may at some point wish to withdraw from treatment. Similarly, intractable inmates may at some point express an interest in pursuing treatment. Given that this will occur, a mechanism must be devised and implemented to deal with these developments. Mechanisms to determine the appropriateness of a change in an inmate's classification status would help protect the integrity of this process.

- Penologists and prison officials must develop and implement methods to ensure that private operators continue to deliver quality treatment programs. This requires contracts that pains-takingly detail the type, quantity, and overall nature of the treatment services that are being purchased. Governmental monitors located in every privately operated prison could further ensure that obligations are being fulfilled (see *McKnight v. Rees*, 1996). Ongoing assessment processes and the collection of performance data related to treatment initiatives would prove especially useful. To reduce concerns even further, only those private operators with a proven history of successful program delivery and who hold appropriate accreditation and recruit and retain staff with suitable professional and educational credentials would be considered for selection.

This concern specifically requires that safeguards be implemented to ensure that governmental jurisdictions take an active and participatory role in treatment processes.

While there are a myriad other concerns that must be addressed with regard to the development of the specialized prison, all problems, regardless of their size or complexity, have a solution. After all, this is precisely the purpose of this book—to identify potential solutions to the many problems confronting the contemporary prison. The idea of prison specialization has now been proposed and, while much is yet to be done, I believe it is worthy of our full consideration.

How Specialization Contributes to the Field of Penology

One of the purposes of this book is to reinvigorate the field of penology. Thus, I have addressed the characteristics of the typical inmate, spoken of the advantages of offender reform, and propounded the merits of innovative and progressive penal thought. As a field of study, penology is certainly overdue for an infusion of innovative and progressive thought, which promotes efficiency and is instrumental in helping us identify ways to maximize the prison's ability to promote public safety. As a proposal, prison specialization contributes significantly to the field of penology by

- raising essential but often ignored questions about the nature and purpose of the contemporary prison,
- challenging the trend toward inmate aggregation,
- identifying and acknowledging the two divergent lines of thought pertaining to contemporary prison operations—normalization and less eligibility,
- recognizing that the ultimate purpose of the prison is to promote community safety via inmate containment and reform,
- recognizing the necessity for classification processes that consider an inmate's security as well as his/her treatment needs,
- recognizing that some inmates are appropriate for treatment while others are not,
- recognizing the value of external performance measures as a way to assess the prison's social value, and

- recognizing that the practice of housing tractable and intractable inmates within the same areas of the prison proves counter-productive to society's well-being.

Several final comments about penology appear appropriate. Penology as a recognized field of interest has all but been abandoned. Few individuals now call themselves penologists. In fact, this label has taken on a negative connotation. As the prison has increasingly adopted a warehousing approach, scholars who formerly identified themselves as penologists are now hesitant to do so. It appears that there are hardly any academicians who want to be associated with an institution that is viewed more negatively now than at any previous time in modern history. Those dedicated scholars who have not abandoned penology find it increasingly difficult to gain access to the prison or obtain information from its officials. Of course, by curtailing access to the prison and its data, correctional administrators are able to effectively shield themselves from research-based criticism. These observations suggest that few individuals are now willing to challenge contemporary penal practice. A prison system that is permitted to operate free of criticism should be a matter of concern, since it is criticism that serves to protect the long-term interests of society. Without a cadre of individuals to critically challenge the nation's correctional leaders, further degradation is a certainty.

Predictions

This chapter opened with the observation that unless changes are made to the prison, it will remain ineffective at promoting the public's long-term safety. Without reform the prison will continue to be guided by those who neither appreciate its broader purpose nor care about its ability to reduce crime rates. Simply put, until reform is undertaken citizens will continue to be plagued by unnecessarily high crime rates. Without reformative measures similar to those exemplified by specialization initiatives, the prison will

- continue to be portrayed negatively within popular culture,
- continue to be perceived negatively by the citizenry,

- continue to be ignored by academia,
- continue to operate unaware of its objectives,
- increasingly adopt a cold and detached approach to its contact with inmates,
- become an institution where inmate mistreatment frequently occurs and is ignored,
- increasingly be staffed by those who have little interest in strategies that promote the public's long-term safety,
- continue to measure its performance by those characteristics that its officials deem appropriate but in reality do little to promote public safety, and
- become less accountable for its actions even when those actions adversely affect inmates and citizens alike.

Collectively, these observations suggest a future for the prison that is quite different from what its original designers envisioned. With an increasingly negative image with which to contend, with fewer penologists to critique contemporary operations, and with the prison's future path left to the fate of an uninformed staff, the prison will do what many governmental enterprises do when left unchallenged—it will expand. I have often stated that the prison is an institution that should work diligently to reduce the need for its very existence. However, the modern prison has taken on a life of its own and, like any living creature, it grows. Unfortunately this growth requires nourishment, and the nourishment the prison seeks is a continuous stream of offenders. Once these offenders have been acquired, the prison denies them treatment, thereby assuring their return. This suggests that the individual inmate is of little consideration to the modern system. Furthermore, these predictions suggest that the future inmate will experience a prison that is extremely cold, harsh, and brutal. The inmate will be buried deep within the prison's catacombs, languishing for years with hardly any activities to occupy his/her daily routine. The intense boredom and lack of positive activity will create the most dangerous prison environment ever experienced. Lack of stimulation and daily challenge leads to frustration that makes inmates violent and the prison dangerous. Once paroled or discharged, the ex-inmate will return to society wholly unprepared to deal with the stresses, strains, and temptations that freedom presents.

Unprepared to deal effectively with others and not ready to locate and maintain employment, the ex-inmate will have little choice but to resort to those coping mechanisms that have proved effective while incarcerated— intimidation and the liberal use of violence. As the prison continues to deteriorate into a cold and detached institution, it will breed an increasingly cold and detached ex-inmate. The prison will become one of the most destabilizing forces in society. Instead of proactively promoting public safety, it will perpetuate crime, making it the antithesis of its former self.

Whenever I tell an audience that the contemporary prison perpetuates crime, I am often asked, "How?" The answer to this seemingly complex question is actually rather simple. The contemporary prison is increasingly becoming an institution of "higher learning." It is there that the intractable inmate teaches criminal techniques to the tractable inmate. Without quality treatment to counter this influence or a staff that is able to shield the tractable inmate from the corrupting influence of the intractable, many inmates become more antisocial and criminally minded while incarcerated. I have personally spoken with numerous inmates who compare their terms of incarceration to attending college. One might sadly observe that both the college and the prison are preparatory institutions (but in much different ways)—the college prepares its students for legitimate careers and the prison its inmates for advanced criminal careers. This is why tractable and intractable inmates must not be allowed to mingle. To do so is counterproductive to the public's long-term interests, and it also places the citizenry at increased risk. Generalized institutional placement as a contemporary penal practice must be discontinued. But as I stated earlier, there is good news: it is not too late for reform. We can again make the prison an institution that focuses on the individual. Such an approach would demonstrate a deep-seated interest in society's well-being. Reform through the creation of the specialized prison would

- force officials to acknowledge the prison's traditional objectives and history,
- require officials to recognize that a value exists in adopting a rehabilitative ideology,
- require that inmates become the focus of the prison's efforts, and
- increase the overall effectiveness of the prison, as evidenced in lower recidivism and crime rates.

Specialization and the changes that it requires would transform the prison into an institution that is ready to take a place of prominence alongside the hospital and school. We must never forget that the prison was originally designed to be a proactive institution. It has unfortunately begun to move in the opposite direction. As the prison has become less proactive in its pursuits, other components of the criminal justice system have become increasingly proactive when dealing with community safety issues. For example, law enforcement agencies in recent years have adopted a community policing approach. One of the hallmarks of community policing is the recognition that for society to be made safer, the police must address problems affecting individual citizens. It is surmised that problems that affect an individual's quality of life will eventually adversely affect the quality of life of others. As as result of addressing issues that affect the individual, both the individual and society benefit. Much like the police, the judiciary has also become more proactive in dealing with community safety issues. For example, the judiciary has been innovative in its creation of "drug courts." A drug court is a specialized forum designed specifically to deal with drug-related offenders and it seeks to address drug issues at the individual level through treatment rather than punishment. This proves more efficient and effective in promoting the community's long-term interests. Both these approaches recognize that when the individual becomes the focus of an altruistic justice system, both the individual and society benefit. Each of these examples typifies a renewed interest of the criminal justice system in ways to increase community safety via the individual. While other components of the criminal justice system are seeking ways to promote the community's safety more effectively, the prison is becoming less proactive and less innovative in its approach. If this trend is to be reversed, specialization is the way forward, since it is both innovative and proactive.

Summary

In this chapter I have asked a serious and thought-provoking question, "Where do we go from here?" There are probably as many answers to this question as there are individuals who will read this book.

Nonetheless, I believe that specialization holds great promise, as it is through specialization that the prison will become more effective in promoting community safety. The beneficiaries of the specialization approach will be the inmate as well as the average citizen. Change is inevitable, and the prison is now ready for change. However, this change must be planned and purpose-driven. Prison reform is no longer optional, especially when we realize that failure to reform means loss of property and, regrettably, even loss of life. Yes, specialization will take time and effort but it will ultimately be worth the investment. When privatization and specialization are linked, as is proposed here, reductions in correctional expenditure will undoubtedly result. With the private sector increasingly holding a greater percentage of our tractable inmate population, it stands to reason that it is the private sector that should assume the role of the "professional" prison. Ultimately it matters very little whether you agree with my premise that specialization holds promise. What is important is an acknowledgment that our citizens deserve more than what they are currently receiving as returns for their investment. While I believe prison specialization will help remedy the many shortcomings of the contemporary prison, surely the debate and discussion that accompany this proposal will heighten awareness about current penal approaches. This may help temporarily stall and perhaps even reverse current trends. We would all do well to remember that the prison is whatever we choose to make it. My sincerest hope is that we choose to make it an institution that is concerned with the success of the inmate and that as a result it becomes an institution that effectively promotes the long-term safety of society. Improvement is always the result of a suggestion, and a suggestion is always the result of a question—so I again ask, "What if . . . ?"

Chapter Highlights

1. Progressive penologists have long searched for ways to improve the prison's ability to promote public safety.
2. The prison's future is not a predestined path and it can and should be altered.

3. Before the prison's path can be altered for the benefit of society, practitioners must become familiar with its history and traditional objectives.
4. While most penologists agree that the prison is in need of change, debate exists about the extent of change needed.
5. A reform ideology humanizes the prison.
6. By not recognizing the importance of inmate reform, prison officials are failing in their duty to promote public safety.
7. Internal measures of prison performance consider characteristics that are largely hidden from the public's view.
8. Internal measures of a prison's performance include the number of months a prison has remained escape-free as well as the number of institutional misconduct reports its staff issue each year.
9. Internal performance measures provide little meaningful information to the average citizen.
10. Recidivism is an external performance measure.
11. External performance measures quantify a prison's achievements in a manner that is easily understood by the average citizen.
12. There are two groups of inmates, those who are changeable (tractable) and those who are unchangeable (intractable).
13. Unchangeable inmates often disrupt and hinder treatment processes.
14. Contemporary prison officials erroneously assume all inmates to be unchangeable.
15. Since all inmates are assumed to be unchangeable, treatment in the modern prison is generally underemphasized, understaffed, and underfunded.
16. Since some inmates desire change while others do not, there must be specialized prisons to deal with each type.
17. Public prisons tend to house serious and dangerous inmates, while private prisons tend to house less serious and less dangerous inmates.
18. Since the private sector houses the less serious and less dangerous inmate, a greater percentage of its prisoner population is believed to be tractable.
19. Prison specialization promotes community safety by emphasizing inmate reform.
20. Prison specialization promotes community safety by eliminating the ability of the intractable inmate to further corrupt the young, impressionable, and less hardened offender.
21. Prison specialization promotes operational efficiency by providing treatment only to those who are tractable.
22. It is not too late; the prison can again become an institution that promotes public safety by focusing upon the needs of the individual inmate.

Discussion Questions

1. How would you improve the prison's ability to promote public safety? What are the similarities (if any) between your proposal and prison specialization?
2. Would you describe the prison's evolution as smooth or can it be characterized by constant change and change-reversal? Explain.
3. Can prisons that adhere to the principle of less eligibility effectively promote public safety? How? What is the relationship, if any, between less eligibility and inmate warehousing? Explain.
4. Does a reform ideology humanize prison operations? Explain.
5. Do you agree or disagree that there are two types of inmates, the changeable and the unchangeable? Explain.
6. From a citizen's perspective, which performance measure, internal or external, proves more informative? Which provides a better measure of the prison's ability to promote community safety? Explain.
7. Are recidivism rates an appropriate performance measure for the custodial prison? Explain.
8. Which sector, the public or private, is better suited to assume the duties of the professional prison? Explain.
9. What advantages does prison specialization provide to the inmate? What advantages does it provide to society? Does specialization present any disadvantages? Explain.

Sources

Archambeault, W., and D. Deis Jr. 1996. Executive Summary—Cost Effectiveness Comparisons of Private Versus Public Prisons in Louisiana: A Comprehensive Analysis of Allen, Avoyelles, and Winn Correction Centers. Baton Rouge: Louisiana State University.

Armstrong, G., and D. Mackenzie. 2003. Private vs. Public Juvenile Correctional Facilities: Do Differences in Environmental Quality Exist?, *Crime and Delinquency*, 49, pp. 542–563.

Bumphus, V., C. Blakely, and M. DeMichele. 2001. Administrative Attitudes about Private Correctional Management. *Prison Service Journal, 134*, pp. 13–16.

Criminal Justice Institute. 2000. *The 2000 Corrections Yearbook—Private Prisons and Adult Corrections.* Middletown, CT.

Index